Complete Library Skills

Grade 3

Published by Instructional Fair
an imprint of
Frank Schaffer Publications®

Instructional Fair

Author: Linda Turrell
Editor: Cary Malaski

Frank Schaffer Publications®

Instructional Fair is an imprint of Frank Schaffer Publications.

Send all inquiries to:
Frank Schaffer Publications
8720 Orion Place
Columbus, Ohio 43240-2111

Complete Library Skills—grade 3

ISBN 0-7424-1953-3

2 3 4 5 6 7 8 9 10 MAZ 11 10 09 08 07

Table of Contents

DISCARDED

Third Graders Use the Library

Until now, you may have been using the library to find books about imaginary things or funny stories. Maybe you chose picture books that were bright and colorful. Or maybe you read every book in your favorite series. You can find all these things in a library. But you can also find much, much more.

Many people use a library to learn about real people, places, and things. In a library, you can find information for a report on the anaconda, read a magazine about mountain climbing, find the population and size of a city, and so much more. The amount of information you can find in a library is endless. And it's all yours to explore!

▶ **Go on a scavenger hunt in your library. Find ten books on real-life (nonfiction) topics that interest you. Write the book titles below. You will share these with your class. Did you all find different books?**

_____   _____

_____   _____

_____   _____

_____   _____

Your Librarian

School librarians are the CEOs of the library. They know where, when, and how everything happens inside their libraries. If a book is checked out, they know who has it. If a book is missing, they start investigating. And if a book is late, they know where to look for it.

But librarians do a lot more than just check out and check in books. Many librarians work with teachers to help choose books that will be useful for reports and projects. Librarians can help students find books within their reading levels. Librarians also show students how to use the online card catalog to search for subjects, books, and authors.

The librarian is also the one who has taught you over the years how to care for a book. She wants to make sure that everyone has a chance to enjoy all of the books, so she takes caring for a book very seriously. And so should you!

A library without a librarian would be like a circus without a ringmaster. The show would not go on!

Name _____ Date _____

What's in a Library?

Most libraries have a section for fiction books. This section contains picture books and make-believe stories. These are usually low to the ground so younger kids can find them.

Most libraries have a large nonfiction section. This section contains books on real subjects, such as animals, places, people, and sports. This is the section you can use when you need information for a report.

Libraries also have a section for magazines. Usually only current magazines can be found here, but your librarian might have older issues for you to look at. Computers can also be found in most libraries. You use a computer to search the online card catalog for a specific book, author, or subject.

▶ **Read each sentence. Use a word from the Word Bank to complete each sentence.**

Word Bank
real
subject
magazines
Libraries
fiction

1. _____ are divided into many sections.

2. I would look in the _____ section to look for an imaginary story.

3. The nonfiction section is where I find books on _____ subjects.

4. I can search the online card catalog for an author, book, or _____ .

5. Current _____ can be found in libraries.

 0-7424-1953-3 *Complete Library Skills*

Mother May I?

You've been assigned to be the library monitor for your school. A bunch of students are wandering the halls. As they come to the door of the library, you need to give them some direction. There are lots of reasons to use a library. Cut out each reason at the bottom of the page. If it is a good reason to enter the library, glue it under the library monitor. If it is not, glue it under the traffic stopper.

Before you begin, write one reason of your own for using the library.

_____

1. I want to learn how to care for plants.

2. I want to run around and scream.

3. I want to practice my basketball moves.

4. I want to draw on books and rip pages.

5. I want to find a book to take home.

6. I want to learn about Chicago, Illinois.

What's in a Title?

Gloria the Goldfish loves to read books. One day she went to the Aquarius Library and found a book titled *How to Avoid Cats*. She found the title page and read the information.

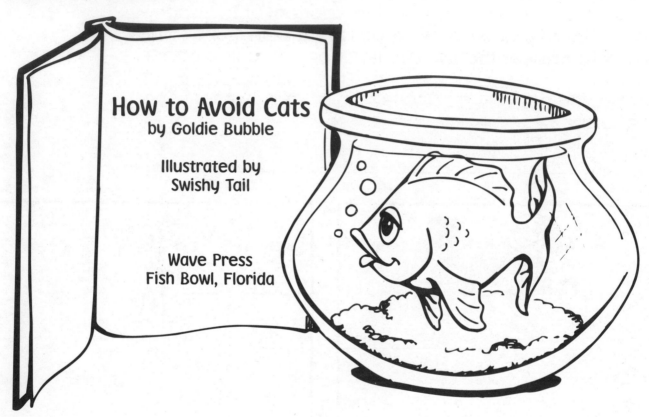

How to Avoid Cats
by Goldie Bubble

Illustrated by
Swishy Tail

Wave Press
Fish Bowl, Florida

➡ **Help Gloria answer the questions below about the book.**

1. Who is the author? _____

2. What is the title? _____

3. Who is the illustrator? _____

4. Who is the publisher? _____

5. Where was the book published? _____

6. Is this book fiction or nonfiction? _____

Name _____ Date _____

Using a Table of Contents

Many book are divided into sections or chapters. The sections are listed in the table of contents. The table of contents shows you the names of the sections and the page numbers where they begin. You can look here to find just what you need.

➤ **The table of contents below is from a book on weather. Use it to answer the questions.**

Table of Contents

Weather Begins with the Sun 4
Measuring Wind 10
Tornadoes and Hurricanes 18
Water, Water Everywhere 25
Rain, Snow, and Sleet 32
Clouds 41
Predicting Weather 50

1. On what page does a chapter on wind begin? _____

2. How many chapters are in this book? _____

3. Which chapter begins on page 18? _____

4. If you wanted to learn how to predict weather, what page would you turn to? _____

5. How many pages are in Water, Water Everywhere? _____

6. Which chapter begins on page 4? _____

7. Which chapter would you read if you wanted to learn about types of clouds? _____

8. About how many pages are in this book? _____

The Table Tells a Lot

Tily Turtle found a book titled *Turtles and Tortoises*. He knows that the table of contents tells him the titles of chapters and where he can find things in a book.

Table of Contents

▶ **Help Tily answer the questions below about where to find things in this book.**

1. How many chapters are in this book? _____

2. In which chapter would you find out who is smarter, the tortoise or the hare? _____

3. On which page does the chapter about prehistoric turtles begin? _____

4. Which chapter talks about the future of turtles in space? _____

5. How many pages are in the chapter about North American turtles and tortoises? _____

There Are So Many Books!

The library has so many books. There are different ways you can go about choosing a book that is right for you.

Choose a book that is at your reading level. To do this, open to a page in the middle of a book. Start reading. For every word you don't know, put up a finger on one hand. If you have five fingers up after reading one page, the book is probably above your reading level. If you don't have any fingers up after reading a page, the book is probably below your reading level and it is too easy for you.

Listen to your teacher or librarian. They know what you like, and they can help you choose a book that is just right for you.

Listen to your friends. Ask them for a book they like. If the book is at your reading level, check it out.

Pull a book from the bookshelf that looks interesting. Read the back cover. Look at the pictures on the cover. Does it look and sound like a book you would like? If so, check it out.

Search the online card catalog by an author, title, or subject. This is a fast and easy way to find a book that might be right for you.

0-7424-1953-3 *Complete Library Skills*

Name _____ Date _____

Choose Your Books Wisely

The library has a lot of books to choose from. Whether you need a book for a report, are learning about a hobby, or want to read for fun, the library will always have a book that is right for you. Look at the following things when deciding if a book is right for you: the title, realistic vs. imaginary art, the length of the book, the amount of words you do and do not know.

▶ **Look at the books below. Match each book with the person who is looking for it. Write the letter of each book on the line.**

1. I like to read mysteries about UFOs. _____

2. I want to learn how to build a kite. _____

3. I like to read about prehistoric times. _____

4. I want to learn about unexplained flying objects. _____

5. I need to read about wind and erosion. _____

6. I like books about dinosaurs that live with people. _____

a.
THE EFFECTS OF EROSION

b.
Can Benny Come Out To Play?

c.
Before We Were Here

d.
Make Your Own Kite

e.
The Light in the Sky

f.
Explaining UFOs

Name _____ Date _____

Name That Book

► **Read each book description below. Make up a title for each one. Then draw a cover to go with it.**

1. This book is for people who want to learn about cheetahs. It includes information about their coats, their diets, and their habitats.

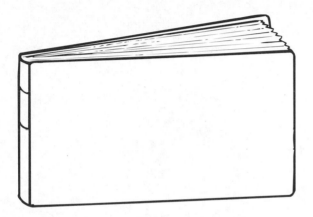

2. This book explains how houses are built. A construction worker shows the steps it takes to build a home.

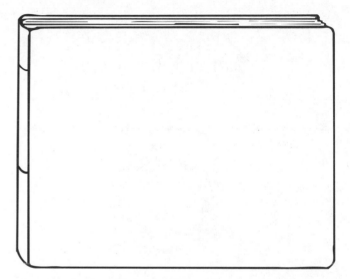

3. This book tells the story of a boy who grows up on a farm. Then one day his family moves and he has to get used to living in a big city.

4. This book describes the life of a circus clown. It is written by a circus clown and includes real pictures of his life on the road.

Name _____ Date _____

Who Needs It?

When looking for different types of books, you should know what to look for. The cover of the book can tell you a lot about what's inside. If the title is silly or funny, you know it is just for fun. If the art looks realistic, it is probably a good book to use for a report.

▶ **Look at the books below. Cut them out and paste them under the student who would check them out.**

I need to find information for my report on insects.

I love reading bug stories.

Name _____ Date _____

Out of Order

To use a library, you have to know that books are placed on bookshelves in a certain order. Some books are alphabetized by the author's last name (fiction). Other books are placed on the shelves in numerical order and alphabetical order (nonfiction books).

▶ **Look at the bookshelves below. They are almost correctly alphabetized by the authors' last names, but some books are out of order. Circle the books that are out of order and draw an arrow to show where they belong.**

A fiction book shows the first two letters of the author's last name on the spine.

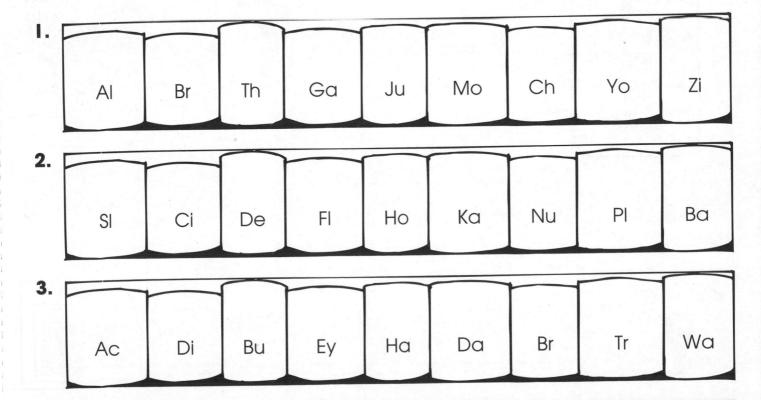

1. | Al | Br | Th | Ga | Ju | Mo | Ch | Yo | Zi |

2. | Sl | Ci | De | Fl | Ho | Ka | Nu | Pl | Ba |

3. | Ac | Di | Bu | Ey | Ha | Da | Br | Tr | Wa |

0-7424-1953-3 *Complete Library Skills*

Name _____ Date _____

Alphabetical Challenge

▶ **Using the Word Bank, write the words in alphabetical order. Solve the riddle by using the letters in parentheses.**

Word Bank
judge
saturate
minimum
final
quip
satellite
cabbage
method
erode
rare
ebony
yearn
paste
hospital
satire
justice
range
host
jolt
radio

_ (_) _ _ _ _ _
_ (_) _ _ _ _
_ (_) _ _ _
_ (_) _ _ _ _
_ _ (_) _ _ _ _
_ _ _ (_)
_ _ (_) _
_ _ _ _ (_)
_ _ _ _ _ (_) _
_ _ _ _ (_) _
_ _ (_) _ _ _ _
_ _ _ _ (_) _
_ _ _ (_)
_ _ _ (_) _
_ _ (_) _ _
_ _ _ _ (_)
_ _ _ _ _ _ _ (_) _
_ _ _ _ (_) _
_ _ _ _ _ _ _ (_)
_ (_) _ _ _

?? ? What is the oldest living thing at 4,900 years old?

_ _ _ _ _ _ _ _ _ _ _   _ _ _ _   _ _ _ _

0-7424-1953-3 *Complete Library Skills*

Poppy's Problem

Poppy has a problem. She can't find her pal, Pokey. Follow the words in alphabetical order to help her find Pokey.

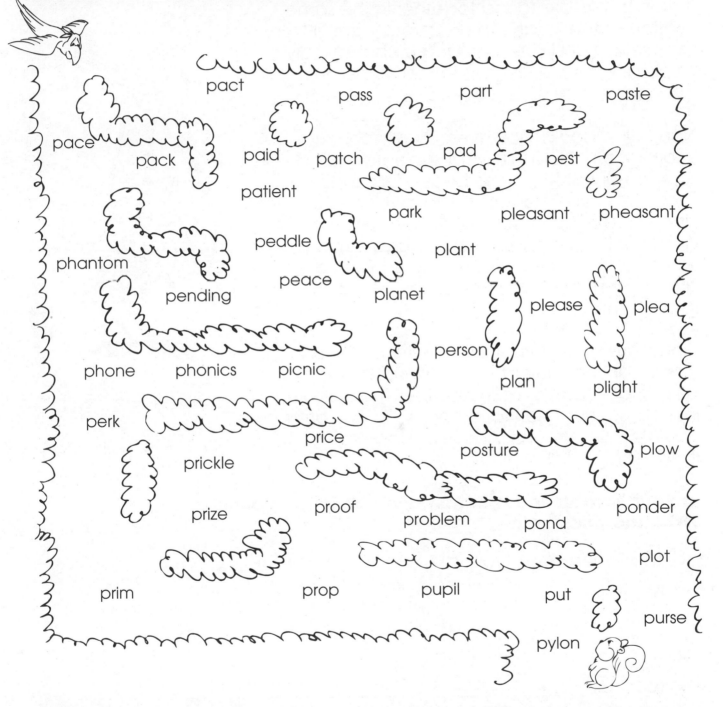

pact   pass   part   paste

pace   pack   paid   patch   pad   pest

patient   park   pleasant   pheasant

phantom   peddle   plant   please   plea

pending   peace   planet   person   plan   plight

phone   phonics   picnic   posture   plow

perk   price   ponder

prickle   proof   problem   pond   plot

prize   prop   pupil   put   purse

prim   pylon

Challenge: Circle the words that did not fall in Poppy's path. On the back of this page, write them in alphabetical order.

Fiction and Nonfiction

A fiction book tells a story of people, places, or things that are all made-up or imaginary. All fiction books are found together in the same section of the library. They have a letter "F" on their spines and are arranged alphabetically according to the first two letters of the author's last name.

Nonfiction books, however, usually contain information about different subjects, such as science or history. These books describe true facts and events about a topic. There are many kinds of nonfiction books. Like the fiction books, all nonfiction books are found together in the same section of the library. These books are arranged numerically according to the subject matter.

Compare these two titles—*Learning About Insects* and *Attack of the Toothless Beaver*. *Learning About Insects* describes facts about insects, so it is a nonfiction book. *Attack of the Toothless Beaver* is a made-up story, so it is fiction.

▶ **In your library, find a fiction and nonfiction book. Write the titles below.**

1. The fiction book I found

is _____.

2. The nonfiction book I

found is _____.

0-7424-1953-3 *Complete Library Skills*

Name _____ Date _____

Your Fiction Book

➤ **Illustrate the cover of your own fiction book. Include a title and the author's name (your name) with your drawing.**

 0-7424-1953-3 *Complete Library Skills*

Your Nonfiction Book

▶ **Illustrate the cover of your own nonfiction book. Include a title and the author's name (your name) with your drawing.**

0-7424-1953-3 *Complete Library Skills*

Fiction or Nonfiction?

▶ **Read each book title and description below.
Write fiction or nonfiction on the line.**

1. *The Chicken and the Weasel* by Arnie Feather. This is the
story of a weasel who helps a chicken remember his
way home. _____

2. *The Planets* by Peter Starry. This book describes the planets
in our solar system. Descriptions and pictures of each planet
are included. _____

3. *Explorers Go to America* by Jim Boat. This book gives the
routes the explorers took to America. Maps and illustrations
are given. _____

4. *Pinky, the French Poodle* by Phil Poof. This is the story of a French
poodle with pink fur. _____

5. *Dinosaurs of Long Ago* by Greg Tail. This book describes the types of
dinosaurs that roamed long ago. _____

6. *Dogs and Their Owners* by Roger Leash. This book describes the types
of ways to train your dog. _____

7. *How to Start an Aquarium* by Sally Swimmy. This book tells you what
to buy and how to put it together. _____

8. *Pokey's Summer Vacation* by Mike Tuxedo. This book tells about how
Pokey the penguin stays cool during the hot summer months.

_____

Fiction Call Numbers

Books have "addresses" just like houses do. A house has an address so people can find it. A book has an address for the same reason. A book's address is called its call number, and it helps people find it on a bookshelf. The **call number** can be found on the book's spine.

If a book is fiction, it will have an F on its spine with the call number. The F stands for **fiction**, and the book will be placed in the fiction section of the library. Fiction call numbers are made up from the first two letters of the author's last name. Fiction books are placed on bookshelves in alphabetical order by their call numbers.

▶ **Look at the examples below.**

Jeff Carpenter wrote *Ants in My House*, a fiction book. If you weren't sure if it was fiction or not, you could look at the spine for an *F*. What two letters do you think you would find under the *F*? The spine of the book would look like this:

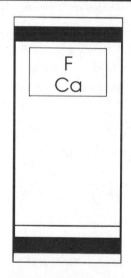

My Night on Pluto was written by Fawn Faraway. It is a fiction book. What two letters make up its call number? Look at its spine. Is it correct?

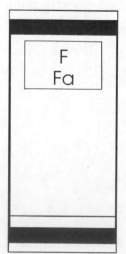

Call Me!

▶ **Look at each fiction book below. Write its call number on the spine next to it.**

1.

2.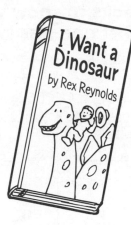

3.

4.

5.

6.

7.

8.

9.

Name _____   Date _____

Order Up!

▶ **Look at the book spines below. They are not in alphabetical order. Figure out what order they should be in. Write 1st, 2nd, and 3rd underneath the books to show what order they would be in on a bookshelf. The first one has been done for you.**

1.

F Ba	F Za	F Ra
1st	3rd	2nd

2.

F Ob	F Eb	F Ab
___	___	___

3.

F Sn	F On	F An
___	___	___

4.

F Ro	F Zo	F To
___	___	___

5.

F It	F At	F St
___	___	___

6.

F Di	F Wi	F Ji
___	___	___

7.

F Br	F Tr	F To
___	___	___

8.

F Pi	F Di	F Mi
___	___	___

9.

F Mu	F Lu	F Pu
___	___	___

10.

F Na	F Ma	F Ha
___	___	___

0-7424-1953-3 *Complete Library Skills*

Musical Books

➤ **Rearrange the books below so they are in alphabetical order. The first one has been done for you. Remember to include the *F* for fiction.**

1.

F Jo	F Po	F Lo		**F Jo**	**F Lo**	**F Po**

2.

F Gl	F Sl	F Kl				

3.

F Mi	F Ri	F Hi				

4.

F De	F Me	F He				

5.

F Ma	F Za	F Ba				

6.

F Fr	F Br	F Gr				

Nonfiction Call Numbers

Nonfiction books have their own section of the library. They will not be found with picture books or story books. Nonfiction books are about all different subjects, such as plants, outer space, people, and machines. Folktales, fairy tales, and poetry are all considered nonfiction.

A nonfiction book has an "address" on its spine that helps you find it on the bookshelf. It is easy to tell the difference between a fiction and a nonfiction book because the nonfiction book has numbers as well as letters (fiction books just have letters). These numbers and letters make up its call number.

The book titled *The Book of Seashells* by Amy Shore has a call number of:

Section of the library—597

Amy Shore—Sh

597
Sh

Name _____ Date _____

How Nonfiction Books Are Arranged

Nonfiction books are arranged on bookshelves according to their call numbers. They are arranged starting with the lowest call number (000) and work up to the highest call number (999). Look at the bookshelf below. These nonfiction books are in order.

133 Ke	220 We	394 Be	420 Se	599 Ar	636 Te	793 Ce	811 Fi	970 Bl

Sometimes more than one book will have the same numbers in their call numbers. When this happens, they are arranged alphabetically by the author's last name (like with fiction books). Look at the bookshelf below. These nonfiction books are in order, also.

599 Gr	599 Zi	636 Te	636 Wi	793 Ce	793 Mo	811 Ca	811 He	811 Se

0-7424-1953-3 *Complete Library Skills*

Arrange the Nonfiction Books

▶ **Put the following nonfiction call numbers in order. If two or more call numbers have the same numbers, look at the letters and arrange them alphabetically. Number them 1–5.**

1. 400 Ta _____
2. 800 Bl _____
3. 900 Br _____
4. 600 St _____
5. 300 Ad _____

1. 400 Wa _____
2. 600 Re _____
3. 500 Al _____
4. 300 Sr _____
5. 200 Be _____

1. 900 De _____
2. 700 Fl _____
3. 500 Ho _____
4. 400 Jo _____
5. 200 Cr _____

1. 470 Sr _____
2. 470 Bu _____
3. 450 Fr _____
4. 420 Fl _____
5. 410 Ma _____

1. 850 Th _____
2. 890 Bu _____
3. 890 Ze _____
4. 830 Gu _____
5. 870 Me _____

0-7424-1953-3 *Complete Library Skills*

Name _____ Date _____

Which Comes First?

➤ **Put the following nonfiction call numbers in order. If two or more call numbers have the same numbers, look at the letters and arrange them alphabetically. Number them 1–5.**

1. 537 Ke _____

2. 536 Or _____

3. 533 Jo _____

4. 535 St _____

5. 533 Tr _____

1. 964 Ta _____

2. 963 Bl _____

3. 965 Br _____

4. 967 St _____

5. 965 Ad _____

1. 757 Br _____

2. 759 Ab _____

3. 759 Pe _____

4. 752 He _____

5. 751 Ca _____

1. 565 Th _____

2. 432 Ki _____

3. 152 Ei _____

4. 384 Ru _____

5. 974 Om _____

1. 565 Br _____

2. 499 Sh _____

3. 384 Ca _____

4. 962 Je _____

5. 499 Zo _____

0-7424-1953-3 *Complete Library Skills*

The Card Catalog

The card catalog contains cards of information about every book in the library. Each book has three cards of information— one each for the author, title, and subject of the book. Each card contains the same information, but the first line of each card is different.

The title card begins with the title of the book.	The author card begins with the author's last name.	The subject card begins with the subject of the book.

Why are there three cards for each book? Well, if you're looking for a book titled *The Truth about Pandas* but don't know the author, you can look at the subject or title cards. Or if you want to find a book by one of your favorite authors but don't know the title, you can look at the author card.

Looking into the Card Catalog

The cards in a card catalog show you the call number, author, title, publisher, place of publication, copyright date, page count, and an annotation (summary) of a book. The cards can show you if the book has illustrations. Look at the three cards below.

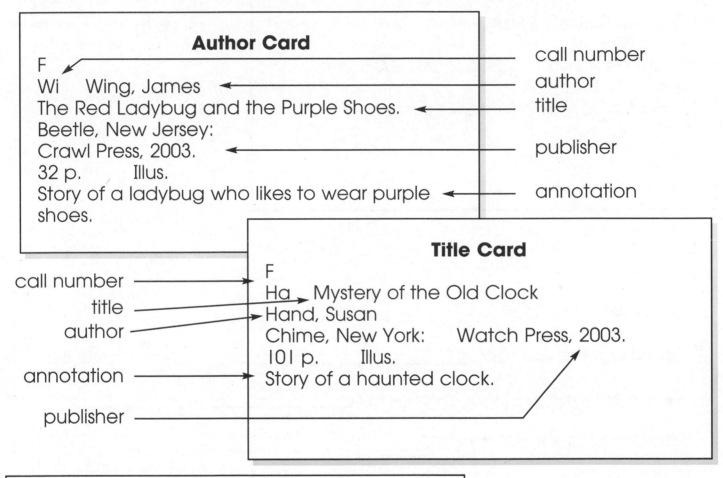

Author Card

F — call number
Wi   Wing, James — author
The Red Ladybug and the Purple Shoes. — title
Beetle, New Jersey:
Crawl Press, 2003. — publisher
32 p.   Illus.
Story of a ladybug who likes to wear purple — annotation
shoes.

Title Card

call number —
title —
author —

F
Ha   Mystery of the Old Clock
Hand, Susan
Chime, New York: Watch Press, 2003.
101 p.   Illus.

annotation —   Story of a haunted clock.

publisher —

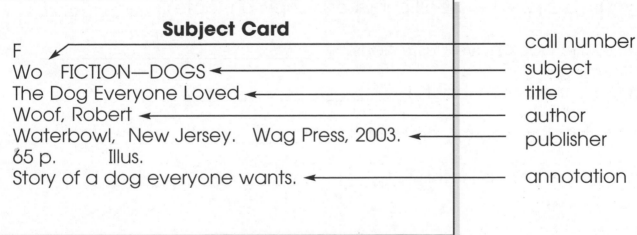

Subject Card

F — call number
Wo   FICTION—DOGS — subject
The Dog Everyone Loved — title
Woof, Robert — author
Waterbowl, New Jersey.   Wag Press, 2003. — publisher
65 p.   Illus.
Story of a dog everyone wants. — annotation

0-7424-1953-3 *Complete Library Skills*

Reading a Card

➡ **Look at the card below. Answer the questions.**

```
F
Po     The Forgetful Frog
Pond, Pamela
Marsh, New York:      Bog Press, 2003.
54 p.        Illus.
Story of a frog who forgets everything.
```

1. What is the call number? _____

2. What is the title? _____

3. Who is the author? _____

4. Where was the book published? _____

5. Who published the book? _____

6. What year was the book published (copyright date)? _____

7. Does the book have illustrations? _____

8. What is the book about? _____

9. Is the book fiction or nonfiction? _____

10. What type of card is this? _____

Name _____ Date _____

Reading a Card

➡️ **Look at the card below. Answer the questions.**

```
F
Ro    Rock, Pete
The Dinosaur Next Door.
Rockville, New Jersey:      Stone Press, 2003.
80 p.         Illus.
The story of the neighborhood dinosaur.
```

1. What is the call number? _____

2. What is the title? _____

3. Who is the author? _____

4. How many pages does this book have? _____

5. What is this book about? _____

6. Where was this book published? _____

7. Is this book fiction or nonfiction? _____

8. Does this book have illustrations? _____

9. What year was this book published (copyright date)? _____

10. Who published the book? _____

Name _____ Date _____

Reading a Card

▶ **Look at the card below. Answer the questions.**

F
Fi FICTION—SEALS
The Seal Who Couldn't Swim
Fin, James
Barkstown, New York:
Whisker Press, 2003.
45 p.   Illus.
Story of a seal who couldn't swim.

1. What is the title? _____

2. What is the call number? _____

3. Is this book fiction or nonfiction? _____

4. Who is the author? _____

5. How many pages does this book have? _____

6. When was this book published (copyright date)? _____

7. What is this book about? _____

8. Does this book have illustrations? _____

9. What is the subject of this book? _____

10. What type of card is this? _____

Write Your Own Card

➡️ **Write a card for one of your favorite books.**

Call
number

Title

Author and title

Place of publication, publisher, copyright date

Pages   Illustrated or not

Summary of the book (annotation)

What type of card did you just write? _____

Name _____   Date _____

Using a Dictionary

Dictionaries can be divided into three sections—
A–H, I–Q, and R–Z. This makes finding words in a
dictionary easier.

```
      H  I      Q  R
       \ |      | /
A ————————————————— Z
```

▶ **Write the letters that the words below would
come between in the dictionary.**

spill	bargain	February	umbrella
_____	_____	_____	_____
piano	eagle	joke	money
_____	_____	_____	_____

When you open a dictionary, you see two words at the
top of each page. These words tell you the first and last
words on each page. These are called guide words
because they help guide you to the words on that page.

▶ **Open your dictionary to a middle page.**

On what page are you? _____
What are the guide words on this page? _____ and _____
Would the word *live* come before, on, or after this page? _____

Open your dictionary to a beginning page.

On what page are you? _____
What are the guide words on this page? _____ and _____
Would the word *dance* come before, on, or after this page? _____

Open your dictionary to an end page.

On what page are you? _____
What are the guide words on this page? _____ and _____
Would the word *violin* come before, on, or after this page? _____

Crossing Guards

➤ **Choose a word from the Word Bank that would be found on the same page as the guide words below.**

Word Bank
- gate
- easy
- story
- tug
- sand
- many
- yams
- rusty
- picture
- ankle
- carrot
- kick

Across
3. tingle–usual
6. bubble–each
7. ear–end
9. rung–saddle
12. jump–king

Down
1. socket–swing
2. open–puddle
4. first–gift
5. lucky–mat
8. add–apple
10. sad–sink
11. wind–yard

Challenge:
Write the words in the Word Bank in alphabetical order.

1. _____

2. _____

3. _____

4. _____

5. _____

6. _____

7. _____

8. _____

9. _____

10. _____

11. _____

12. _____

0-7424-1953-3 *Complete Library Skills*

No Beans About It

➡ **Look at the entry words and guide words below. Decide if the entry word comes before, on, or after the page with those guide words. Write your answer on the blank.**

Entry Word	Guide Words	Before, On or After
1. ridiculous	reverse–ridicule	_____
2. rough	round–royal	_____
3. opposite	orange–orchid	_____
4. combine	color–crust	_____
5. season	scoop–seat	_____
6. noxious	nozzle–nurture	_____
7. enjoy	echo–emcee	_____
8. alien	alike–allot	_____
9. tribe	track–tribute	_____
10. atoll	agony–antelope	_____
11. grimy	Greek–grid	_____
12. willow	wild–wind	_____
13. lunge	lure–luxury	_____
14. depart	department–deposit	_____
15. liter	link–litter	_____
16. accept	academy–accent	_____
17. pillar	pillage–pinch	_____
18. next	nervous–newt	_____

Challenge: What are the guide words for *jelly bean* in your dictionary?

_____ and _____

Now That's Salty!

▶ **Look at the entry words and guide words below. Decide if each entry word is found before, on, or after the page with the guide words. Write your answer on the line.**

Before, On, or After	Entry Word	Guide Words
1. _____	tidy	title–tool
2. _____	scare	run–sad
3. _____	dizzy	cobra–dry
4. _____	earth	early–effort
5. _____	eclipse	easy–echo
6. _____	harbor	hard–hero
7. _____	air	aim–better
8. _____	angry	across–also
9. _____	donkey	doing–drift
10. _____	exit	extra–fancy

What body of water contains so much salt that even a fish can't live in it?

▶ **To find the answer:**

Write the first letter of each entry word that came **before** the guide words.

___ ___ ___

Write the first letter of each entry word that came **on** the same page as the guide words.

___ ___ ___ ___

Write the first letter of each entry word that came **after** the guide words.

___ ___ ___

▶ **Using your dictionary, find three entry words listed above that came before or after the guide words. Write the entry word and its guide words.**

Entry Word		Guide Words
1. _____		_____
2. _____		_____
3. _____		_____

Summer Syllables

Dictionaries contain a lot of information about words. You can find out how many syllables a word has by looking in a dictionary. To show the number of syllables a word has, spaces are put between syllables.

▶ **Look at the dictionary entries below. How many syllables does each word have? Write your answer on the line.**

Number of Syllables

1. _____ **ask** /'ask/ **v.** I. to pose a question
2. _____ **com e dy** /'kom ĭ dē/ **n.** I. a humorous performance
3. _____ **head** /'hed/ **n.** I. the upper part of the body
   v. I. to go in a certain direction
4. _____ **lit ter** /'lit ər/ **n.** I. garbage **v.** I. to throw garbage in the wrong place
5. _____ **me di um** /'mē dē əm/ **n.** I. something in the middle
6. _____ **o val** /'ō vəl/ **adj.** I. having the shape of an egg
7. _____ **plen ty** /'plen tē/ **n.** I. an ample amount 2. enough
8. _____ **to mor row** /t 'mär ō/ **n.** I. the day after today

Color the graph to show the number of syllables in each word.

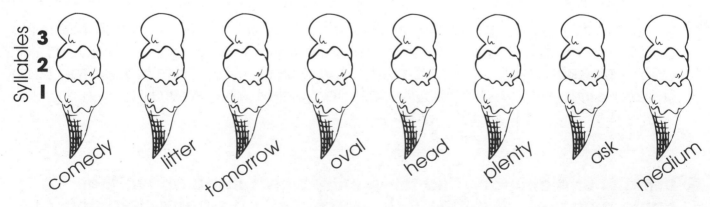

Syllables
3
2
I

comedy   litter   tomorrow   oval   head   plenty   ask   medium

Math Challenge:

(_____ x _____) + _____ = _____
(two-syllable words) (one-syllable words) (three-syllable words)

Sylla-Graph

▶ **Shade in the graph below to show the number of syllables in each word.**

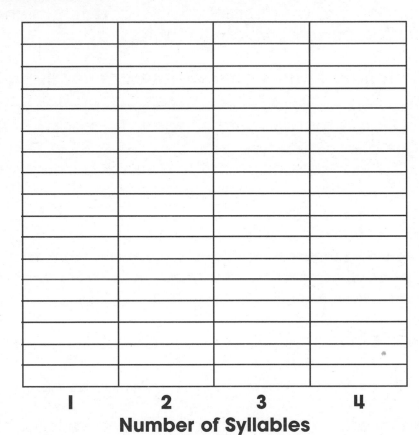

watermelon
breakfast
servant
buffalo
arch
aggressive
victim
column
history
significant
margin
debilitate
pilot
compulsory
cucumber
leisure
sketch

| 1 | 2 | 3 | 4 |

Number of Syllables

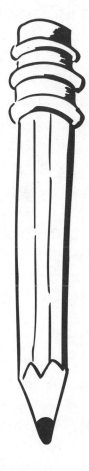

Choose two two-syllable words, two three-syllable words, and two four-syllable words from the list above. Write the words on the lines below. Show each syllable separated by a dash. Check your answers in your dictionary and write the page number of the entry on the line.

Word	**Syllables**	**Dictionary Page**
1. _____	_____	_____
2. _____	_____	_____
3. _____	_____	_____
4. _____	_____	_____
5. _____	_____	_____
6. _____	_____	_____

What Kind of Word Is It?

A dictionary can show you whether a word is a noun, verb, adjective, or adverb. Before the definition, you will see **n**, which stands for *noun*, **v**, which stands for *verb*, **adj.**, which stands for *adjective*, or **adv.**, which stands for *adverb*.

▶ **Look at the dictionary entries below. Then answer the questions.**

---

ape /'āp/ **n.** I. a large monkey with no tail **v.** I. to copy or mimic

land /'land/ **n.** I. the solid surface of the earth 2. a country **v.** I. to cause to come to rest 2. to arrive 3. to strike or meet a surface

skate /'skāt/ **n.** I. a boot with a metal blade or wheels 2. a large fish in the ray family **v.** I. to glide on skates

---

I. *Skate* can be used as a _____ or a _____.

2. As a verb, *ape* means _____.

3. As a noun, *skate* can mean _____ or _____.

4. How many definitions of *land* are given in the verb form? _____

5. Write a sentence using *land* as a noun.

_____

▶ **Use your dictionary to find two words that can be used as a noun or a verb. Fill in the blanks below.**

Word	Page Number
I. _____	_____
2. _____	_____

0-7424-1953-3 *Complete Library Skills*

A Fly with Many Meanings

▶ **Look at the dictionary entry below. Then answer the questions.**

fly /'flī/ **n.** 1. the act of flying 2. a baseball hit high in the air 3. an insect 4. a fishing lure **v.** 5. to move through the air with wings 6. to travel in an airplane 7. to pass quickly 8. to cause to float in the air

1. How many noun definitions are given for *fly*? _____

2. How many verb definitions are given for *fly*? _____

3. How many definitions in all are there for *fly*? _____

▶ **Read the story below. On the lines, write the number of the definition that fits.**

A Fly's (____) Tale

A young fly (____) bought a ticket to fly (____) to his aunt's house in Dallas. When the plane was late, he decided to fly (____) there himself. He was moving along quite nicely when he heard people cheering. He looked down just in time to see a fly (____) ball rising from a baseball field. He reached out and grabbed it. The fans went wild. Soon he was at his uncle's house. "Time sure does fly (____) when you're having fun!" he thought.

Write a sentence using the word *fly* with as many different definitions as you can.

_____

_____

 0-7424-1953-3 *Complete Library Skills*

Words in the Round

➤ **Use a dictionary to decide if each word below is a noun, verb, or both. Cut out the words. Glue them where they belong. Words that can be both a noun and a verb belong in the middle circle.**

Challenge: On the back of this paper, write two sentences for each word in the middle circle. Use the word as a noun and as a verb.

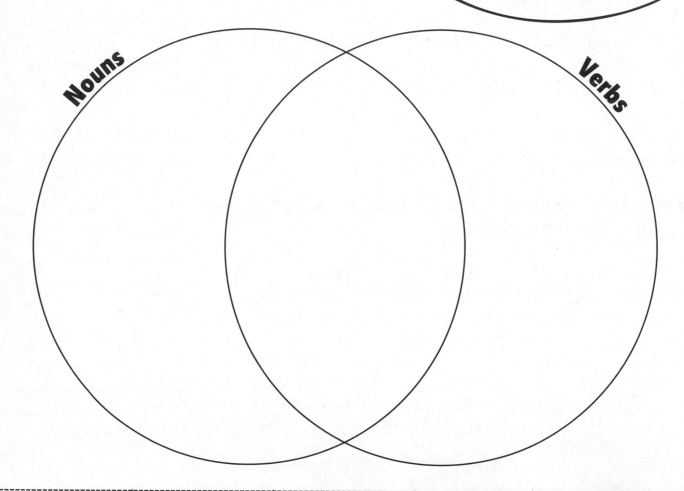

color	rabbit	history	puppy	bird
sail	dew	sweep	draw	buy
hobby	hand	go	say	dime
motel	trap	grow	mop	waste

0-7424-1953-3 *Complete Library Skills*

Animal Crackers

➡️ **Look up each word below in your dictionary. Write the page number on which you found the word and its part of speech. Then write the base word.**

Word	Page	Part of Speech	Base Word
1. basketful	_____	_____	_____
2. untimely	_____	_____	_____
3. lingering	_____	_____	_____
4. hostess	_____	_____	_____
5. wallpapered	_____	_____	_____
6. unending	_____	_____	_____
7. holidays	_____	_____	_____
8. aggravation	_____	_____	_____
9. unutterable	_____	_____	_____
10. librarian	_____	_____	_____
11. energetic	_____	_____	_____
12. inescapable	_____	_____	_____

On the lines below, write the base words that have one, two, and three syllables.

One Syllable	**Two Syllables**	**Three Syllables**
_____	_____	_____
_____	_____	_____
	_____	_____
		_____

Which animal's tongue can weigh more than an entire elephant?

To solve the riddle, use the first letter of each word in the lists above.

__ __ __   __ __ __   __ __ __ __
(one-syllable list) (two-syllable list) (three-syllable list)

Name _____ Date _____

What Are Encyclopedias?

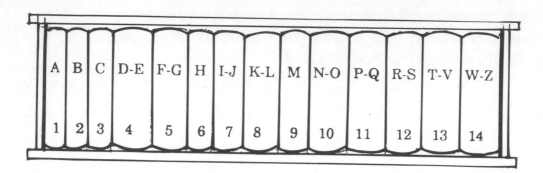

Encyclopedias are large books that contain information about people, places, and things. Encyclopedias are found in sets, like the one above. The volumes are arranged alphabetically. Each volume features information on subjects that start with the same letter. For example, you would look in Volume 3 if you wanted to learn about Canada or cheese. Some volumes contain information on subjects that start with more than one letter. For example, Volume 8 contains information on subjects that start with the letters K–L. You would look in Volume 8 if you wanted to learn about landforms. What other volumes above contain information on subjects that start with more than one letter?

_____

Encyclopedias have guide words to help you find what you are looking for. These are at the top of a page, and they show you the first and last entries on a page. Anything in between these two words alphabetically can be found on these pages.

To find the volume that you need, look on the spines of the encyclopedias. The spine of an encyclopedia shows you which letter of the alphabet the book contains information about. It also shows you the volume number so that you know where it belongs on the bookshelf. For example, if you wanted to learn about Rome, you would pick up Volume 12 from the bookshelf. Volume 12 contains subjects that start with the letters R–S. Which volume would you pick up if you wanted to learn about photosynthesis? _____

Name _____ Date _____

Where Would You Look?

An encyclopedia is filled with information about people, places, and things. A set of encyclopedias contains many books, or volumes. Each volume has information about subjects that start with the same letter. They are arranged alphabetically.

➤ **Look at this set of encyclopedias. Where would you look to find information on the subjects below? Write the volume number for each subject on the line.**

A	B	C-Ch	Ci-Cz	D	E	F	G	H	I	J-K	L	M	N	O-P	Q-R	S	T	U-V	W-X-Y-Z
1	2	3	4	5	6	7	8	9	10	11	12	13	14	15	16	17	18	19	20

1. airplanes _____

2. birds _____

3. spiders _____

4. China _____

5. glaciers _____

6. dinosaurs _____

7. explorers _____

8. Earth _____

9. tides _____

10. The Hubble space telescope _____

11. igloos _____

12. the Concorde jet _____

> How many volumes does this set of encyclopedias have?
>
> _____

A Wealth of Information

You can use an encyclopedia to learn about deserts, Africa, the circulatory system, Pluto, and much more. Encyclopedias also contain information about famous people. When looking for information about a certain person, use the first letter of his or her last name when deciding which volume to look in. For example, if you wanted to learn about Robert E. Lee, you would look for the volume that contains subjects that start with the letter *L*.

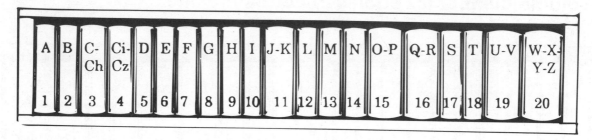

A	B	C-Ch	Ci-Cz	D	E	F	G	H	I	J-K	L	M	N	O-P	Q-R	S	T	U-V	W-X-Y-Z
1	2	3	4	5	6	7	8	9	10	11	12	13	14	15	16	17	18	19	20

▶ **Look at the set of encyclopedias. Next to each subject below, write the volume number for the encyclopedia you would use.**

1. the Dead Sea _____

2. Benjamin Franklin _____

3. Bosnia _____

4. microscopes _____

5. Edgar Allen Poe _____

6. eels _____

7. Ronald Reagan _____

8. protein _____

9. hydrogen _____

10. friction _____

11. Vincent Van Gogh _____

12. polio _____

0-7424-1953-3 *Complete Library Skills*

Name _____ Date _____

So Much Information

Encyclopedia volumes are arranged on bookshelves in alphabetical order. Most information can be found by looking under the letter of the subject you are looking for. However, a person can be found by using the first letter of his or her last name. You would look in Volume K to find Martin Luther King. Along with information, you will notice that some entries have pictures, illustrations, or maps to help you better understand the subject you are studying.

▶ **Match the subjects below with the correct encyclopedia volumes. Write the letter of the volume on the line.**

Subjects

1. Yemen _____

2. quartz _____

3. James Monroe _____

4. levers _____

5. aircraft carriers _____

6. Lou Gehrig _____

7. carbon _____

8. tarantulas _____

Volumes

a. M 10   b. P–Q 13   c. A 1   d. Y–Z 19

e. L 9   f. C 3   g. T 16   h. G–H 7

Volumes of Information

Encyclopedias are filled with useful information. One encyclopedia contains information on countless subjects. For example, Volume B could have information on everything from bees and bugs to Boston and Brazil.

► **Look at the subjects below. Cut them out and glue them under the encyclopedia volumes in which you would find them. Remember: If you are looking for a person, look at the first letter of his or her last name.**

C	L	M

Mayflower Compact	Chile	licorice	capillary	Mount Rushmore
legume	Anton Chekhov	Massasoit	cement	Madeleine L'Engle

Name _____ Date _____

Places Everyone

Baxter is planning a summer trip. He wants to visit several states, but he's not sure which ones. All he knows is that he wants to visit the capital of each state he goes to.

▶ **Help Baxter plan his trip by using an encyclopedia to look up the states below. On the lines, write the capital of each state and two interesting sites that he might want to see.**

	Capital	**Interesting Sites**
Maryland	_____	_____ _____
Colorado	_____	_____ _____
Illinois	_____	_____ _____
Virginia	_____	_____ _____
Texas	_____	_____ _____
Michigan	_____	_____ _____
New York	_____	_____ _____

On the back of your paper, write a paragraph about two interesting sites in your state.

 0-7424-1953-3 *Complete Library Skills*

Where in the World?

Reference materials, such as encyclopedias, can be used to get information from for a report. When you find information that you want to write down, write only key words and phrases. Do not copy sentences word-for-word from the encyclopedia. Create sentences of your own using the facts you have written down.

▶ **Choose a state to research. Find the following information using an encyclopedia.**

The state I'm studying is _____.

1. An important fact from its history

   _____

2. Its size in square miles _____

3. Its population _____

4. Two products that are produced here _____

5. Its motto _____

6. Its state bird _____

7. Interesting places to visit

   _____

   _____

▶ On a separate sheet of paper, write a paragraph or two about the state you chose. Include all of the information from above.

Reference Material Information

_____   _____
Title of article   Encyclopedia

_____   _____
Volume   Page(s)

Snooping Around

Encyclopedias are a good place to look for information about a famous person. You can learn about a figure from history, such as King Henry VIII, or someone a little more contemporary, such as Maya Angelou.

▶ **Choose a person about whom you would like to learn more. Look him or her up in an encyclopedia. Find the following information:**

The person I'm studying is _____.

1. Where and when he/she was born

_____

_____

2. Where he/she grew up _____

3. Why he/she is famous _____

_____

_____

4. Any other important information

_____

_____

▶ On a separate sheet of paper, write a paragraph or two about the person you chose. Include all of the information from above.

Reference Material Information

_____   _____

Title of article   Encyclopedia

_____   _____

Volume   Page(s)

U.S. States and Presidents

Across
4. What is the main agricultural product in Kansas?
5. What is the state bird of Lincoln's birthplace?
6. What river is near President Franklin Roosevelt's birthplace?
7. Thomas Jefferson was born in what state?
8. What President followed Theodore Roosevelt into the White House?
9. What state became a state when Theodore Roosevelt was in office?
10. What is the smallest state in the United States?

Down
1. Andrew Jackson died in what city?
2. What is the capital of the state where Abraham Lincoln was born?
3. The President who followed Lincoln into the White House was born in what city?

Name _____ Date _____

Web of Information

▶ **Use an encyclopedia to find information about the following subject:**

_____

Using the web below, record important information about your subject. You may add more circles if needed.

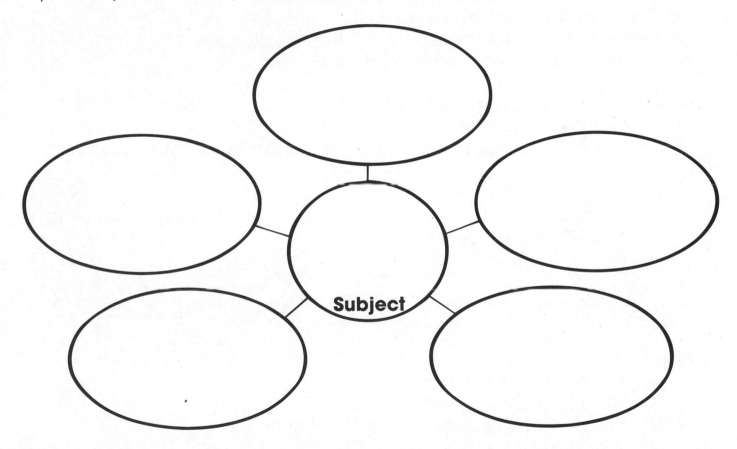

Subject

▶ On a separate sheet of paper, write a few paragraphs about your subject. Include your information from above.

Reference Material Information

_____   _____
Title of article   Encyclopedia

_____   _____
Volume   Page(s)

Name _____ Date _____

What's Another Word For ...?

Sometimes the same word keeps popping up in your head. You want to tell someone to have a good day, but you don't want to use the word *good*. This is where a thesaurus can come in handy. A **thesaurus** is filled with words that have similar meanings (synonyms). For example, if you looked up the word *good* in a thesaurus, you might see the words *great, splendid, superb, decent,* and *wonderful*. These are all synonyms for the word *good*. And just like a dictionary, the words can be found in alphabetical order.

Sometimes words can be used in different ways to mean different things. For example, the word *bug* can be used as a noun and as a verb. Look at the thesaurus entry below.

bug
  1. insect, creepy-crawly
     There's a **bug** crawling on my leg.
  2. to annoy, irritate, aggravate, get on your nerves
     Don't **bug** me!
  3. a virus, fault, defect, problem
     There's a **bug** in the computer program.
  4. to put a listening device in, to listen in
     The police could **bug** the telephones.

▶ **Write a sentence of your own using the word** *bug*.

_____

How Do I Say ...?

Just as a baseball coach might send in a substitute pitcher to make a game better, you might "send in" a substitute word to make your writing better. When you need to find a substitute word, look no further than your thesaurus. Look at the sentence below:

The children climbed to the top of a cliff.

Look in your thesaurus for another word for *cliff*. Write your new sentence below.

The children climbed to the top of a _____.

Do you think you can improve the sentence even more? Now look in your thesaurus for another word for *climbed*. Write your new sentence below.

The children _____ to the top of a _____.

▶ **Read each sentence below. Use a thesaurus to fill in the blank in each sentence with a synonym for the word underneath the line. Read your sentence out loud to make sure the word you have chosen works in the sentence.**

1. I have to _____ at 5 A.M. to catch my flight.
            go

2. I _____ brussel sprouts.
         hate

3. My brother played a _____ trick on me.
                              mean

4. Jenny acts so _____ when she throws a tantrum.
                          young

5. My dad's socks give off an awful _____ .
                                              smell

   0-7424-1953-3 *Complete Library Skills*

The Thesaurus Brontosaurus

Bernie Brontosaurus has written a note to Bernice, his lovely bride, but he doesn't think it is good enough to give her.

➤ **Help Bernie rewrite his note. Use a thesaurus to find synonyms for each blank space.**

My _____ Bernice,
       dear

  Oh, how I miss you! Every _____ I think of you when I get up.
                         morning

I miss your _____ _____ . I miss your _____
            pretty   mouth   shiny

eyes. The sound you make when you _____ _____
                                     eat   bushes

always gives me goose bumps.

    Why did you have to _____ ? I know it's only for a
                         leave

_____ amount of time, but just one day is too long to be
  little

without you. When you come back, you will see how much I've missed

you. I've cleaned up the _____ just the way you like it. I've
                   house

_____ and folded all of the laundry that was in a _____
  scrubbed   pile

on the floor. I've even made a _____ of your favorite fern soup.
                            pot

Your 136th birthday is right around the _____ , and I have
                                 bend

something _____ I want to give you. You'll just have to wait
          special

and see what it is!   Your _____ ,
                                            love

                                            Bernie

0-7424-1953-3 *Complete Library Skills*

What Is an Almanac?

An **almanac** is a collection of information and facts for people of all different walks of life. In an almanac, you might find information on the tides, weather forecasts, current events, calendars, presidents, religions, health, historical anniversaries, and so much more.

Almanacs are updated and changed every year to reflect current events. Since the late 1700s, farmers have been using almanacs to schedule the planting of their crops, and people living near oceans have found the tide tables helpful. Almanacs can also include tables and charts about the planets, eclipses, longitude, and latitude that might be helpful to sailors on ships.

Today, almanacs contain a larger variety of facts than years ago. They can include recipes, information on gardening, animals, wedding traditions, pets, consumer trends, nature, and so much more. There are also many almanacs that now have Internet websites that contain loads of fun facts, tips, stories, this day in history facts, questions of the day, local forecasts, and more.

► Check out these almanac websites for information on, well, almost anything:

www.almanac.com

www.worldalmanacforkids.com

www.worldalmanac.com

www.farmersalmanac.com

 0-7424-1953-3 *Complete Library Skills*

Online Almanacs

Almanacs can be found in most school libraries. You will find them in the reference section, along with the dictionaries and encyclopedias. You also have access to almanacs through the Internet. The almanacs on the Internet are usually updated daily with weather forecasts, horoscopes, questions, tips, and much more.

▶ **For practice using online almanacs, answer the following questions.**

World Almanac for Kids at www.worldalmanacforkids.com

1. How old is the universe? _____

2. What were a few of Harry S. Truman's early careers
   before becoming President of the United States?_____
   _____

3. Who was the NBA's Most Valuable Player in 1997? _____

4. Who invented the zipper? _____

5. What famous people do you share a birthday with? _____

The Farmers Almanac at www.farmersalmanac.com

1. What is the gardening tip of the day? _____
   _____

2. What dates will there be a full moon this year? _____
   _____

The Old Farmer's Almanac at www.almanac.com

1. What happened on this day in history?_____
   _____

2. Find a recipe for something that sounds good to you.
   Write the name of it on the line. _____

3. What is happening this month with the moon and stars?_____
   _____

What Is an Atlas?

An **atlas** is a book filled with maps. It is a reference book, just like a dictionary, encyclopedia, thesaurus, and almanac. It is a good place to look for information.

An atlas shows two types of maps. The first is a physical map, which shows the physical features of a country, such as rivers, deserts, mountains, plains, and lakes. The second type of map is a political map. A political map shows boundaries and important cities. An atlas also has an index in the back to help you locate a map you are looking for.

▶ **Use an atlas to help Kayley Koala answer the questions below.**

1. What is the name of your atlas? _____

2. On what page would you find the state in which you live? _____

3. On what page would you find a physical map of Australia? _____

4. On what page would you find a political map of Europe? _____

5. List three countries that you can find on a political map of Europe.

   _____

   _____

6. On what page would you find a political map of France? _____

7. What is the capital city of France? _____

8. Find a physical map of the United States. What is the largest

   mountain range? _____

   Where is it located? _____

Exploring Egypt

➤ Look at each topic below. If you would use a dictionary to find the information, color the canteen orange. If you would use an encyclopedia, color the canteen blue. If you would use a thesaurus, color it red. If you would use an atlas, color it green. And if you would use an almanac, color the canteen yellow.

the population of Egypt

the life of King Tut

the weather in Egypt

physical features of the Sahara Desert

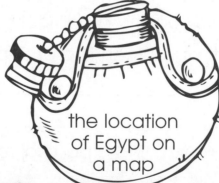

the location of Egypt on a map

parts of speech of the word desert

another word for hot

the spelling of mummification

background information on the pyramids

Name _____ Date _____

The Dewey Decimal Classification® System

Can you imagine what it would be like to look for a book in a library and not have any idea where to find it? It would take all day to find just one book.

Many years ago, this problem really existed. Nonfiction books were not arranged by subject. A librarian named Melvil Dewey thought that something needed to be done about it. In 1876, he created a system of organizing nonfiction books by subject so that they were easy to find. Mr. Dewey divided all nonfiction books into ten sections and gave them all numbers. These numbers are placed on the spines of nonfiction books. Each section contains books on the same subject. This system is called the Dewey Decimal Classification® system.

▶ **Look at the sections and their numbers below. In your library, find a book that belongs in each section. Write the title on the line.**

Sections	Numbers	A Book in This Section
Reference	000-099	_____
Philosophy	100-199	_____
Religion	200-299	_____
Social Science	300-399	_____
Language	400-499	_____
Science	500-599	_____
Useful Arts	600-699	_____
Fine Arts	700-799	_____
Literature	800-899	_____
Geography/History	900-999	_____

000–099 The Reference Section

Each section of the Dewey Decimal Classification® system is broken down into subsections. Lyle the Llama wants to learn more about the first section of this system—the reference section. This section includes encyclopedias, periodicals, and other books that contain information on many subjects. These books are numbered 000-099.

000 Reference Materials

010 Bibliography & Catalogs

020 Library & Information Sciences

030 General Encyclopedias

050 General Serial Publications

060 General Organizations & Museology

070 Journalism, Publishing, & Newspapers

080 General Collections

090 Manuscripts & Book Rarities

▶ **Go to the Reference section of your library (000–099). List books that you find in this section below.**

_____ _____

_____ _____

_____ _____

_____ _____

_____ _____

100–199 Philosophy & Psychology

Willy the Wise Owl is a very logical thinker. He is always thinking about things for hours at a time. He even makes lists of pros and cons when he has to decide on something. Naturally, Willy's favorite section of the nonfiction books is the Philosophy and Psychology section. This section contains books about the mind and feelings.

100 Philosophy & Psychology

100 Metaphysics

120 Epistemology, Causation, Humankind

130 Paranormal Phenomena & Arts

140 Specific Philosophical Viewpoints

150 Psychology

160 Logic

170 Ethics

180 Ancient, Medieval, Oriental Philosophy

190 Modern Western Philosophy

Go to the Philosophy & Psychology section of your library (100–199). List books that you find in this section below.

_____   _____

_____   _____

_____   _____

_____   _____

_____   _____

200–299 Religion & Mythology

Penelope the Winged Horse wanted to learn more about her legendary ancestor Pegasus. In Greek mythology, Pegasus was a beautiful winged horse. You can learn more about Greek mythology by looking in the Religion and Mythology section of the library (200–299).

200 Religion & Mythology

210 Natural Religion

220 Bible

230 Christian Theology

240 Christian Moral & Devotional

250 Local Church & Religious Orders

260 Social & Ecclesiastical Theology

270 History & Geography of Church

280 Christian Denomination & Sects

290 Other & Comparative Religions

▶ **Go to the Religion & Mythology section of your library (200–299). List books that you find in this section below.**

_____   _____

_____   _____

_____   _____

_____   _____

300–399 Social Sciences

Tomelia Turkey likes reading about holidays. Her favorite section of the nonfiction books is the Social Sciences section. In this section, she can read about education, government, legends, fairy tales and folk tales, holidays, and much more. Tomelia found her favorite holiday under Dewey call number 394.

300 Social Sciences
310 Statistics
320 Political Science
330 Economics
340 Law
350 Public Administration & Military Science
360 Social Pathology & Services
370 Education
380 Commerce, Communication, & Transportation
390 Customs & Folklore

▶ **Go to the Social Sciences section of your library (300–399). List books that you find in this section below.**

_____ _____

_____ _____

_____ _____

_____ _____

_____

0-7424-1953-3 *Complete Library Skills*

Name _____ Date _____

400–499 Language

Luke the Toucan has a problem. All of his friends in the rainforest call him "Big Mouth" because he talks so much. This hurts his feelings, but he loves to talk. In fact, he wants to learn how to speak French, German, Spanish, and other foreign languages so that he can talk to anyone who passes by his tree. He spends most of his days with his beak in books from the Language section of the library (400–499).

400 Language
410 Linguistics
420 English & Anglo-Saxon Languages
430 German
440 French—Romance Languages
450 Italian, Romanian, Rhaeto-Romantic Languages
460 Spanish & Portuguese Languages
470 Latin
480 Greek
490 Other Languages

➤ **Help Luke find books on the languages below. Write the titles and Dewey call numbers on the lines.**

Greek _____   Spanish _____

German _____   Romanian _____

French _____   Latin _____

English _____   Japanese _____

500–599 Science

Ali the Allosaurus lived almost 160 million years ago during the Age of Reptiles. The Allosaurus was one of the largest meat-eating dinosaurs of its time. Libraries did not exist during this time, and Melvin Dewey certainly hadn't been born yet. So Ali could not read about her species or other dinosaurs that roamed the earth. If she had been around after Mr. Dewey created his system, she would have looked in the Science section to learn about dinosaurs and more (500–599).

500 Science

510 Mathematics

520 Astronomy & Allied Sciences

530 Physics

540 Chemistry & Allied Sciences

550 Sciences of Earth & Other Worlds

560 Paleontology

570 Life Sciences

580 Botanical Sciences

590 Zoological Sciences

▶ **If Ali roamed the earth today, what books would she find in the Science section of the library? List some books below.**

_____   _____

_____   _____

_____   _____

_____   _____

 0-7424-1953-3 *Complete Library Skills*

600–699 Useful Arts

Bucky Beaver spent too much time pulling Becky Beaver's tail in class and didn't pass his dam-building test. He has one more chance to learn how to build a dam before he is sent to lumberjack camp. Help him find books in the Useful Arts section of the library that will teach him what he needs to know (600–699). Books in this section teach you life skills. While you are there, make a list of other books that you find in this section.

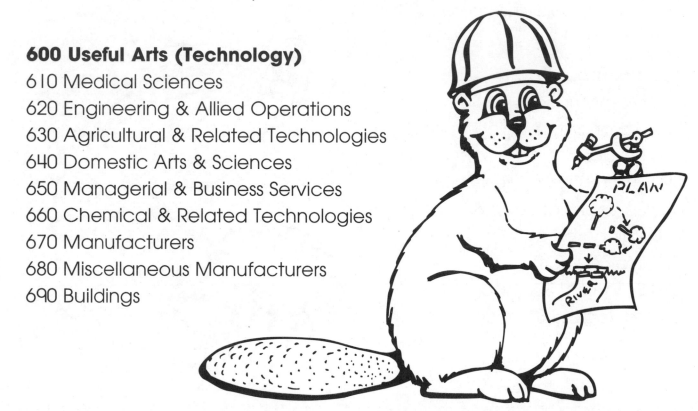

600 Useful Arts (Technology)
610 Medical Sciences
620 Engineering & Allied Operations
630 Agricultural & Related Technologies
640 Domestic Arts & Sciences
650 Managerial & Business Services
660 Chemical & Related Technologies
670 Manufacturers
680 Miscellaneous Manufacturers
690 Buildings

▶ **Look in your library to find books in this section. List them below.**

_____   _____

_____   _____

_____   _____

_____   _____

         0-7424-1953-3 *Complete Library Skills*

700–799 Fine Arts

Germaine the Giraffe wants to learn how to paint. But he is frustrated because he is always taller than the easel he has to paint on. He is convinced that there must be a book for giraffes in his situation. He needs to look in the Fine Arts section of the library (700–799). This section contains books on art, music, sports, and hobbies.

700 Fine Arts
710 Civic & Landscape Art
720 Architecture
730 Plastic Arts—Sculpture
740 Drawing, Decorative, &
      Minor Arts
750 Painting & Paintings
760 Graphic Arts—Prints
770 Photography & Photographs
780 Music
790 Recreational & Performing Arts

▶ **Look through the Fine Arts section of your library. List some hobbies, sports, music, and art that you can learn about.**

_____   _____

_____   _____

_____   _____

_____   _____

_____   _____

Name _____ Date _____

800–899 Literature

Toucan Luke has learned how to speak in different languages. Now he wants to read books in other languages. He needs to look in the Languages section of the library (800–899). This section contains American and foreign literature, as well as plays, poems, and essays.

800 Languages
810 American Literature in English
820 English & Anglo-Saxon Literature
830 German Literature
840 French Literature
850 Italian, Romanian, & Rhaeto-Romantic Literatures
860 Spanish & Portuguese Literatures
870 Latin Literature
880 Greek Literature
890 Literature of Other Languages

▶ **Go to the Languages section of your library. Find a book for each language below. Write the title and Dewey call number of the book on the line.**

English _____ German _____

French _____ Romanian _____

Japanese _____ Latin _____

Greek _____ Spanish _____

0-7424-1953-3 *Complete Library Skills*

Name _____ Date _____

900–999 Geography & History

Now that Toucan Luke has learned how to speak and read in different foreign languages, he wants to learn about the countries in which the languages are spoken. He is especially excited to learn more about South America, his home country. To do this, he must go to the Geography and History section of the library (900–999). Here he can learn all about the continents and countries of the world.

900 Geography & History
910 Geography—Travel
920 Biography, Genealogy, & Insignia
930 History of the Ancient World
940 History of Europe
950 History of Asia
960 History of Africa
970 History of North America
980 History of South America
990 History of Other Parts of the World

▶ **Look in the Geography and History section of your library. Find books about the places below. Write the titles and Dewey call numbers on the lines.**

South America _____   Quebec _____

North America _____   China _____

India _____   Mexico _____

Bosnia _____   Italy _____

Exploring the Sciences

Petey was raised by a pack of badgers and wants to learn more about himself. He is old enough to be out on his own now, and he wants to do what other dogs do. He never liked eating mice and rodents, but he's not sure what he is supposed to eat.

Petey found the section he should look in—Science (500–599). Then he realized that the section is divided into even more sections.

Help Petey learn about himself and the world around him. Look at each book title below. Write the Dewey call number next to each book. Use the chart below and your library to help you.

1. The Cardinal Family _____

2. How to Train Dogs _____

3. The Life of a Fly _____

4. Alligator Homes _____

5. Gorillas _____

6. Ants and Termites _____

7. The Mussels in the Sea _____

8. The Complete Book of Worms _____

9. Looking at Microscopic Animals _____

10. Face to Face with a Tuatara _____

11. Meet the Cephalopod Family _____

12. Be a Zoologist _____

590 Zoological Sciences
591 Zoology
592 Invertebrates Protozoa
593 Mollusks and Related
594 Other Invertebrates
595 Insects
596 Chordates/ Vertebrates
597 Cold-Blooded Vertebrates
598 Birds
599 Mammals

Match the Dewey

The Dewey Decimal Classification® system divides nonfiction books into ten sections.

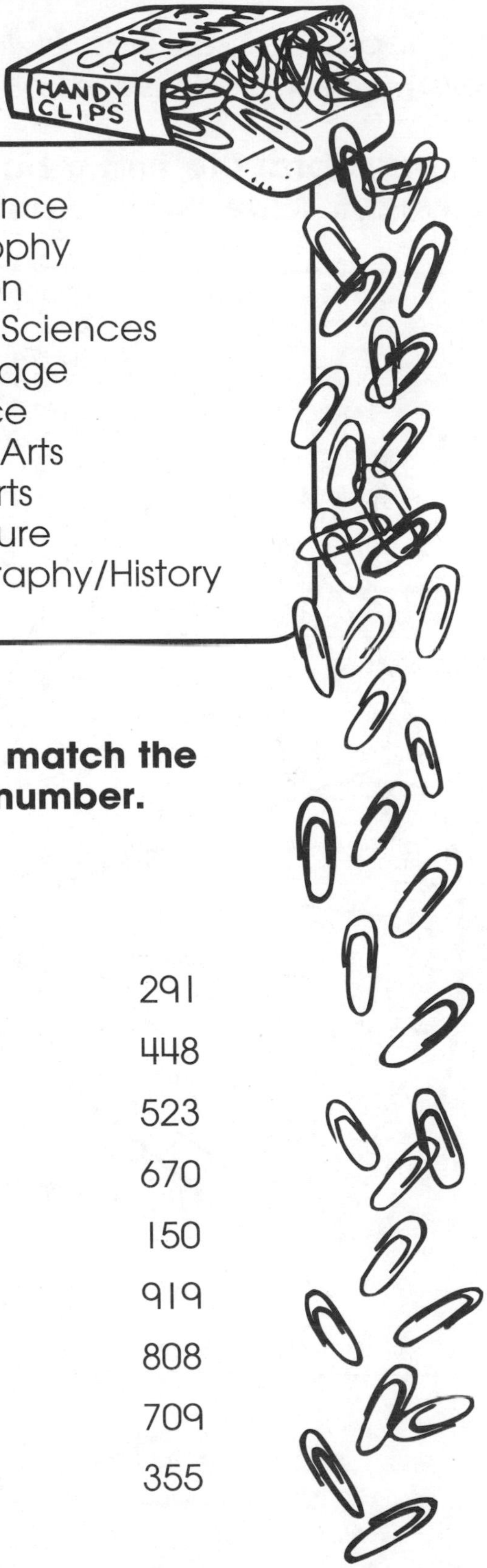

000–099	Reference
100–199	Philosophy
200–299	Religion
300–399	Social Sciences
400–499	Language
500–599	Science
600–699	Useful Arts
700–799	Fine Arts
800–899	Literature
900–999	Geography/History

➤ **Use your library and the chart above to match the book titles below to the correct Dewey number. Draw a line to connect them.**

Book Titles

The Invention of the Paper Clip	291
Journey Through the Solar System	448
Famous Poems	523
World Religions	670
Ancient Roman Art	150
Let's Learn French	919
All About the Mind	808
Training to Be a Soldier	709
Antarctica at a Glance	355

Name _____ Date _____

The Dewey Decimal Classification® Wheel

Each spoke on the wheel below stands for a section of the Dewey Decimal Classification® system. There are ten sections.

▶ **Use your library to find a book that fits into each category of the wheel. Write the title and author of each book in the wheel.**

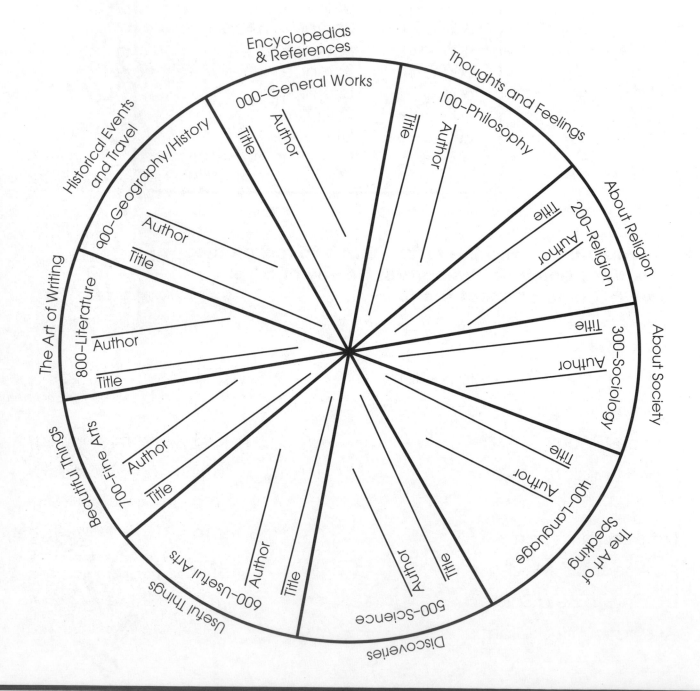

Name _____ Date _____

Genres of Literature

No matter what you're in the mood to read, you can always find a book that is just right in the library. You can find books that teach you things, make you laugh, tell you about a person's life, make you tap your foot to a rhythm, or explain something about the real world. Books come in many different genres. A genre is a type of book.

▶ **Look at the web below. It shows you some genres that you will find in your library.**

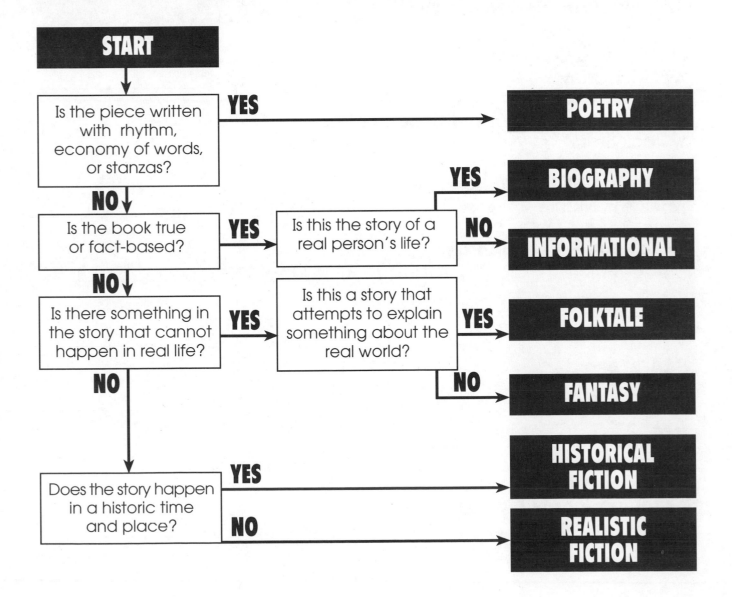

START

Is the piece written with rhythm, economy of words, or stanzas? — **YES** → **POETRY**

NO ↓

Is the book true or fact-based? — **YES** → Is this the story of a real person's life? — **YES** → **BIOGRAPHY**
Is this the story of a real person's life? — **NO** → **INFORMATIONAL**

NO ↓

Is there something in the story that cannot happen in real life? — **YES** → Is this a story that attempts to explain something about the real world? — **YES** → **FOLKTALE**
Is this a story that attempts to explain something about the real world? — **NO** → **FANTASY**

NO ↓

Does the story happen in a historic time and place? — **YES** → **HISTORICAL FICTION**
Does the story happen in a historic time and place? — **NO** → **REALISTIC FICTION**

Name _____ Date _____

Biographies & Autobiographies

Books that are written about people's lives are called either biographies or autobiographies. A book is a biography if it is written by someone other than whom the book is about. If it is an autobiography, then the author wrote about his or her life.

► **Read each book title below. Is it a biography or an autobiography? Write your answer on the line.**

My Life as a Carpenter
by I. M. Handy

This book is a(n) _____.

The 36th President of the United States
by Jack Star

This book is a(n) _____.

I Won One Million Dollars!
by Luck E. Man

This book is a(n) _____.

Bill Lawson—A Life in Exile
by Zoe Tucker

This book is a(n) _____.

Everyone Wants My Job
by Julie Stevens

This book is a(n) _____.

Katy's Life
by Margaret Melody

This book is a(n) _____.

Cynthia Chandelier—Exposed
by Doug Deeper

This book is a(n) _____.

Searching for My Mother
by Carolyn Bridges

This book is a(n) _____.

Name _____ Date _____

Read a Biography

A biography is a book about a person's life written by another person. It might include information such as when and where he or she was born, how many people were in his or her family, and the impact that he or she had on the world. Biographies include facts and true information and are often used for reports or projects about famous people.

► **Choose a biography on a person you want to learn more about. After you have answered the questions below, use this sheet to prepare a report that you will give on the person you have chosen.**

My biography report is on _____.

Title of book _____

Author _____

Copyright date _____

Date of birth _____ Place of birth _____

What was this person's childhood like?

_____

_____

_____

What is this person known for?

_____

_____

Did he or she have to overcome obstacles/trouble in life? _____
If so, what? _____
If you could meet this person in real life, what would you like to ask him or her?

_____

_____

List two things you learned about this person.

_____

_____

 0-7424-1953-3 *Complete Library Skills*

Match the Biographies

You can read about someone's life in a biography. This is a book that is written by someone other than the subject of the book, but the author has done research so that he or she can write about the person.

▶ **Look at the book titles on the left. They are biographies. Find the book cover that matches each book on the right. Draw a line to connect the cover with the book that it goes with.**

Football's Reigning King

General Robert E. Monocle

She Did It—You Can Too!

Their Journey to the Top

Your Autobiography

An autobiography is similar to a biography. It is a book about a person, but it is written by the person that it is about. Your autobiography can be written only by you.

➤ **Now it's time to write your autobiography—no one else can write it for you. Write your answers to the questions below. Use the information to prepare your autobiography that you will share with your class.**

Full name _____

Date of birth _____ Place of birth _____

Members in your family _____

_____

What your childhood has been like _____

_____

Most memorable moment _____

_____

Favorite memory _____

_____

Favorite vacation _____

_____

Things I have done to contribute to my family, our school, our community

_____

_____

_____

_____

It Could Really Happen!

Have you ever read a story and thought, *This could really happen*? This kind of story is called **Realistic Fiction**.

Realistic fiction ...
- is a story that could happen, even if events are extraordinary or improbable.
- is a story set in current times, not in historical times.
- is a story with a setting that is believable and vivid because it is described well.
- is a story with well-developed characters that are described through words, actions, and thoughts.
- has action or plot development that really holds the reader's interest.
- is a story with characters and conflicts that are well-developed.
- offers the reader the opportunity to look at his or her own feelings and actions, as well as others' feelings and actions.
- demonstrates that people are in charge of their own lives and can bring about change through their own actions.
- demonstrates that all people share common experiences.

➤ **The book titles below are for realistic fiction books. But the titles are incomplete. Finish each book title so that each book is realistic fiction.**

1. The Day My Cat _____

2. My Trip to the _____

3. My Dad, Alex, Lindsey, and the Green

_____

4. The Icy Cold _____

5. Help! I'm Trapped in a _____

Is It Real?

Realistic fiction books seem like they could be real. They feature real characters with real problems and situations. One of the reasons people like reading realistic fiction is because they can imagine the situation happening to them.

▶ **Look at the books below. If a book is realistic fiction, draw its cover. If it is not realistic fiction, cross out the word in the title that makes it imaginary. Replace that word with a word that makes the book realistic fiction. Then draw its cover.**

I'm Grounded!

My Pet Rhinoceros

The Librarian Who Flies

One Cold, Wintry Day

I Ate 120 Bananas!

The Metal-Eating Contest

Historical Fiction

Do you like reading books that take you back to a different period in history? Books that help you travel back to a time in history are called **Historical Fiction**.

Historical fiction ...
- is a fictional story set during an important historical period.
- combines a realistic story with factual information.
- includes some characters who might be fictional and others who might be real people who lived during that historical period.
- has real and fictional events mixed into the plot.
- is a reading opportunity to learn more about a specific historical period or event.
- brings history alive through the reader's interest in the characters and through details of everyday life, historical events, and differences in attitudes and beliefs.

Look at the books below. They are all historical fiction books.

Number the Stars by Lois Lowry
Magic Tree House series by Mary Pope Osborne
Little House series by Laura Ingalls Wilder
Secret Garden by Frances Hodgson Burnett
Sing Down the Moon by Scott O'Dell

Name _____ Date _____

A Glimpse into the Past

Historical fiction books give us the rare opportunity to feel what it must have been like to live during a certain period of history. Through these books we can learn about medieval times, pioneer days, the civil war era, ancient Egyptian civilizations, the westward movement, and much more.

▶ **Choose three historical fiction books from your library. Fill in the blanks below about each book.**

Title _____ Author _____

Time period _____ Setting _____

Historical details _____

_____

Similarities between this time period and the present time

_____

_____

Title _____ Author _____

Time period _____ Setting _____

Historical details _____

_____

Similarities between this time period and the present time

_____

_____

Title _____ Author _____

Time period _____ Setting _____

Historical details _____

_____

Similarities between this time period and the present time

_____

_____

Name _____ Date _____

Folktales and Fairy Tales

Folktales and **fairy tales** are stories that people share with friends and family generation after generation. Can you think of a story you have been told by a parent or grandparent?

Folktales ...

- are stories that have been shared orally and passed down for generations.
- are often fairy tales, a category that includes actual stories about fairies, but also stories that use traditional folktale plots and elements.
- are stories with generic settings, often beginning "once upon a time" and "long ago and far away."
- are stories in black and white, with characters that represent either good or evil (the wicked witch, the good prince, the bad wolf). Characters tend to be flat and not described in detail, such as, "the wise old woman" or "the happy king."
- feature a main character who is often alone or isolated in some way, such as Little Red Riding Hood, Hansel and Gretel, or Cinderella.
- often feature a problem that has a life-or-death outcome.
- reward good and punish evil. These tales often have a "happily ever after" ending.

Some well-known folktales and fairy tales are ...

Cinderella	Rumpelstiltskin	Little Red Riding Hood
The Princess and the Pea	Hansel and Gretel	Rapunzel
Jack and the Beanstalk	Snow White	Sleeping Beauty
The Frog Prince	The Little Mermaid	

Writing a Folktale

Writing a folktale is a difficult job unless a student already knows a tale passed down from generations before. Since most students do not know a folktale well enough to expand on it, this activity is designed to offer students a chance to show their knowledge of folktale elements and to have some fun, too. Students will write a "fractured" folktale using the structure of a well-known folktale and adding humor to it.

Writing in this genre offers
- the opportunity to understand the concept of literary elements and archetypes.
- a chance to demonstrate knowledge and attempt parody.

1st Step
Students listen to various fractured folktales and discuss the added element of humor. Examples of fractured folktales to real aloud:
- Point of view: *The True Story of the Three Little Pigs* by Jon Scieszka
- Culture: *The Three Little Javelinas* by Susan Powell
- Overall: *The Three Little Wolves and the Big Bad Pig* by Eugene Trivizas

2nd Step
Students use the organizer on page 88 to help them begin organizing their folktale.
- Remind them that their folktale must have a beginning, middle, and end.

3rd Step
Students write their folktale.
- Make sure students are using the information from their organizers. Check student organizers before students start to write their folktales.

Name _____ Date _____

Fractured Folktale Graphic Organizer

Setting

Good characters

Major problem

Bad characters

Magic number(s)

Beginning

First event

Second event

Magic or trickery

Repetition

Final event

Ending

0-7424-1953-3 *Complete Library Skills*

Name _____ Date _____

Fantasy Land

Sometimes it's fun to read a book that takes you on a magical journey or an exciting out-of-this-world experience. When you read a book like this, you have to be willing to leave reality, for just a little while, and travel into your imagination. These types of books are called **Fantasy** books.

A fantasy ...
- includes something that cannot really happen.
- can include an imaginary world.
- offers the reader's imagination an escape from reality.
- offers the reader a message for living in today's world.

In high fantasy ...
- a fantastical world, such as Oz or Narnia, is presented.
- time is flexible; real-world time is nonexistent.
- the main character believes his or her experiences are real.
- the central conflict is between good and evil.

In science fiction ...
- the fantasy is based on scientific theories and technological inventions.
- there are often moral and ethical questions.
- the setting is often in the future.

A few examples of fantasy books are
Harry Potter series by J. K. Rowling
The Eternity Code by Eoin Colfer
The Complete Chronicles of Narnia by C. S. Lewis
Bridge to Terabithia by Katherine Paterson
Tuck Everlasting by Natalie Babbitt

0-7424-1953-3 *Complete Library Skills*

Prompt the Imagination

Some students have a hard time letting go of reality and venturing into the world of imagination. When students need a little help, try the following activities.

Rev Up the Imagination
Provide a short prompt to your students and allow them to finish the story. Give prompts that allow the fantastical elements to change based on characters, settings, or events. For example: You're walking through a dark forest and all of a sudden a frantic foobling jumps in front of you. Have your students describe the foobling and tell what happens next. *Or* try this one: As you and a friend are sipping your favorite milkshakes, your friend is suddenly sucked into the straw and out of sight. What do you do?

Partners Point/Counterpoint
Students work as partners to stretch their imaginations by playing a writing game. The first player makes up the beginning of a story. The next player expands on what the first player wrote, adding fantastical elements. The first player then takes another turn. For example:

First player: When the alarm clock went off, I fell out of bed.

Second player: The floor had turned into a bed of marshmallows overnight, and it broke my fall. But now I was stuck in the marshmallowy goo and couldn't move.

First player: I yelled for my mom, and she came running. Before I could stop her, she ran right into the goo and was stuck from the knees down.

Second player: The heat from our bodies was making the marshmallow expand, and it was slowly rising. We had to do something, and fast!

This activity can continue as long as the students are interested. Share some of the stories to encourage reluctant participants to use their imaginations.

Imagine a World Where...
In this activity, students become the creators of their own worlds, like C. S. Lewis or Maurice Sendak. Give the class the assignment of creating an imaginary world. Each student must explain in words as well as drawings what his or her new world is like. Ask questions to get students started. Questions could include:
- What does the landscape look like?
- Who lives there?
- How do the beings communicate?
- What is the history of this world?
- What is the weather like there?
- What do the beings look like?
- How do they get from one place to another?
- Who is in charge of the world?

For an additional activity, have each student write a story about his/her life and create a diorama or model of his/her world. Share the models in class.

Informational Books

Informational books can be a wonderful source of facts and information.

Informational books ...
- are filled with information and facts related to a specific topic, though sometimes theories are also included.
- use content-specific vocabulary.
- use imagery and figurative language to compare the known with the unknown.
- have a specific format including some or all of the following: table of contents, picture or diagram captions, subheadings, sidebars, glossary, index, and bibliography.

Combination books ...
- are fictional storylines used as a means of presenting true information. A popular example of this is the *Magic School Bus* series by Joanna Cole. These books provide information to children in an interesting and exciting manner by combining fiction and factual information.

▶ **Choose an informational book from your library.**
Answer the following questions about your book:

Title of book _____ Author _____

Copyright date _____ Number of pages _____

Does your book have

a table of contents? ☐ Yes ☐ No Page number _____

a glossary? ☐ Yes ☐ No Page number _____

an index? ☐ Yes ☐ No Page number _____

a bibliography? ☐ Yes ☐ No Page number _____

subheadings? ☐ Yes ☐ No

picture captions? ☐ Yes ☐ No

Animal Information

➤ **Choose an animal to research.
Take notes on this page.**

What animal have you chosen?

_____

What is its scientific name?

_____

What type of creature is it? Circle one.

Reptile   Amphibian   Mammal   Bird   Fish   Invertebrate

Describe how this animal looks. _____

_____

What makes this animal unique?_____

Where does this animal live?_____

What does this animal eat? _____ Where is it in the food

chain?_____

Write three interesting facts about your animal. _____

_____

_____

Is this animal endangered? _____ If so, from what? _____

_____

Could this animal be a pet? _____ Why or why not? _____

_____

Poetry

Poems can be a lot of things. They can be beautiful, funny, sad, rhyming, nonrhyming, and much more. A lot of poems that you read rhyme, but that doesn't mean they have to. Many famous poems don't have one rhyming word in the entire poem.

Poetry ...
- uses rhythm in words, phrases, and lines, often creating a musical effect.
- can rhyme or be free verse.
- plays with language, sounds, meanings, etc.
- is often written in stanzas, or groups or lines.
- uses economy of words; offers the essence, not the whole thing.
- uses figurative language such as similes, metaphors, and personification.
- uses imagery; the poet paints a picture in the reader's mind.
- can evoke strong feelings and emotions; is powerful.
- leaves the reader with something to think about; is memorable.

Verse ...
- generally has rhyme and rhythm.
- offers little or no depth of emotion.
- does not leave the reader with an important thought or lingering emotion.
- provides poetry readiness.

▶ **What is one of your favorite poems? Write the title and author on the line.** _____

Why is this poem one of your favorites?_____

_____

_____

_____

Suggested Poetry List

The following is a list of recommended poems to use when introducing poetry to your students.

Category \ Title and Author	"The Pickety Fence" by David McCord	"Eight-Oh-Three" by Carol Diggory Shields	"There Was an Old Man with a Beard" by Edward Lear	"Have You Ever Seen?" (Anonymous)	"Smokescreen" by Charles Ghinga	"The Swing" by Robert Lois Stevenson	"The Creature in the Classroom" by Jack Prelutsky	"Jimmy Jet and His TV Set" by Shel Silverstein	"Mummy Slept Late and Daddy Fixed Breakfast" by John Ciardi	"Fog" by Carl Sandburg	"America the Beautiful" by Katharine Lee Bates	"Who Has Seen the Wind?" by Christina Rossetti	"Since Hanna Moved Away" by Judith Viorst	"Four Little Foxes" by Lew Sarett	"Slithergadee" by Shel Silverstein	"Mother Doesn't Want a Dog" by Judith Viorst	"Fueled" by Marcie Hans
Rhythm Word Music	●	●	●	●	●	●	●	●	●		●	●	●	●	●	●	●
Rhyme	●	●	●	●	●	●	●	●	●		●	●	●	●	●	●	
Plays with Language	●	●		●	●										●		
Stanzas		●		●		●	●	●	●		●	●	●	●		●	
Economy of Words		●		●	●	●		●	●	●	●	●	●	●			●
Figurative Language or Imagery	●	●	●		●	●	●		●	●	●	●	●	●	●	●	
Strong Feelings							●				●		●	●			●
Something to Think About	●			●		●					●		●	●		●	●

0-7424-1953-3 Complete Library Skills

Where Do I Look?

When you use a library for research, you have many options of places to look for information, such as encyclopedias or almanacs. Each type of book is different, and so you would choose to use them for different reasons. The web shows you the types of books you can use for researching a topic and the differences between the books. Keep in mind that many subjects can be found using any or all of the research materials listed in the web.

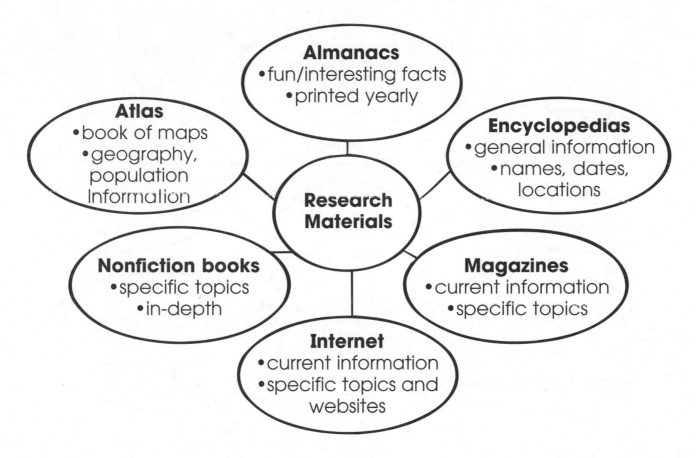

▶ **What sources could you use to find information for a report on Michigan?**

_____

What sources could you use to find information for a report on baseball?

_____

If you were using an atlas, what might you be doing a report on?

_____

   0-7424-1953-3 *Complete Library Skills*

Name _____ Date _____

Researching a Country

Your teacher has assigned you the following research project:

_____
                                    Country

▶ **Using the graphic organizer below, take notes on your assigned country. Use multiple research materials.**

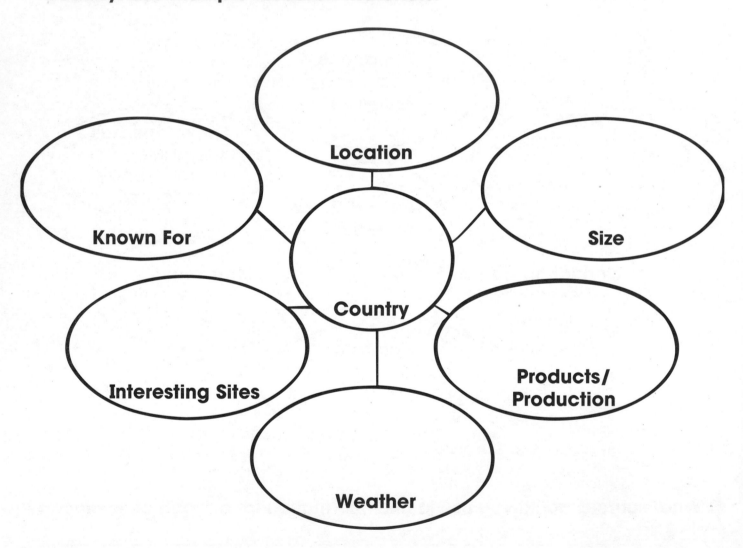

Bibliography of research materials

_____

_____

_____

Researching an Inventor

Where would we be today without the light bulb or the toaster? What would life be like if the radio had not been invented?

► **Research a famous inventor. Learn about his or her childhood and the invention that made him or her famous. Use the graphic organizer below in which to write your notes. Use a variety of research materials.**

Inventor

Date of birth

Place of birth

Family members

Childhood

Invention

How the idea came about

Effect it had on the world

Bibliography of research materials

_____

_____

_____

Researching a Biome

The earth is covered with different types of biomes. Some are hot and humid. Others are cold and treeless.

► **Choose two biomes that interest you. Use at least three resources in which to find your information. Compare and contrast the two biomes using the Venn diagram below. Write the name of each biome above its circle.**

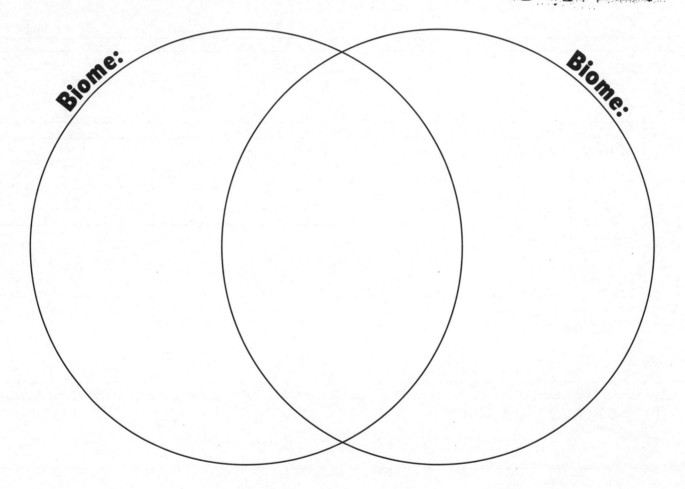

Biome:

Biome:

Bibliography of research materials

_____

_____

_____

Name _____ Date _____

Researching Emotions

During a day, you probably experience a range of
emotions, from happy to sad, from excited to let-down.

▶ **Do some research on human emotions. Use multiple
research materials to find information on the feelings
and emotions we experience. Fill in the chart below
with the information you have found. Then write
about an experience you've had with that emotion.**

Emotion	Something I've Learned About This Emotion	My Experiences	
		The Cause	**My Reaction**
Anger			
Sadness			
Happiness			
Fear			
Excitement			
Nervousness			

Researching Your Favorite Food

If you could have anything to eat right now, what would it be? A cheeseburger and fries? A big steak? Or maybe a piece of cheesecake?

➤ **Think of your favorite food. You have probably eaten a lot of it. Now learn about it. What country did it come from? When was it created and by whom? What different variations of it are there? Use different sources to learn all about your favorite food. Record your information below.**

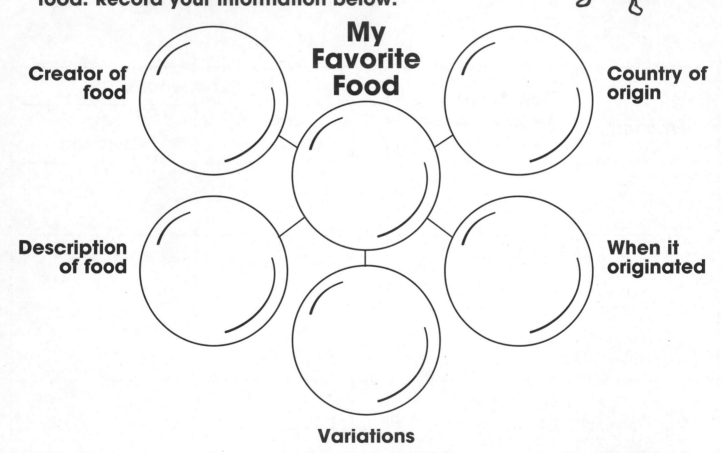

My
Favorite
Food

Creator of
food

Country of
origin

Description
of food

When it
originated

Variations

Bibliography of research materials

_____

_____

_____

0-7424-1953-3 *Complete Library Skills*

Name _____ Date _____

The Electronic Card Catalog

Many libraries no longer have card catalog drawers that are located in the library. Many libraries have switched their card catalog drawers over to electronic

card catalogs. These are accessible through computers in the library, and they are very similar to card catalogs drawers.

Electronic card catalogs can be searched by subject, title, author, keyword, or call number. The information that is found on a card from the card catalog drawer can also be found in the results of an electronic search. Look at the results from an electronic search below.

551.5
FRA   **Title:** The Effects of Wind / by Dennis Brindell Fradin; consultant, James L. Rasmussen
Author: Fradin, Dennis B.
Series: Weather!
Series: Fradin, Dennis B. Weather!
Published: Chicago: Children's Press, c1983.
Description: 63 p.; illus. (some color)
Notes: Includes index.
Notes: Discusses causes and effects of wind. Also includes information about the Dust Bowl and other historical windy events.
Elec. Access: Internet sites about Wind.
Subject: Wind Storms—United States.
Subject: Wind—United States.
Subject: Wind.
Subject: Disasters.
Subject: Weather.
Subject: Erosion.

Name _____ Date _____

Searching the Electronic Card Catalog

In order to find information on a book that you are looking for, you have to know how to search through the electronic card catalog. There are a few different ways to search for a book.

How will you search?

⦿ Search by title: If you know the title of the book, simply enter it into the search field.

⦿ Search by author: If you don't know the title but you know who wrote the book, enter the author's name into the search field. This should bring up all books written by this author. Then you can choose your book from that list.

⦿ Search by subject: If you are looking for books on a certain subject for a report or project, you can search by subject to see what books your library has on the subject. Then you can browse through the books and their descriptions to determine which books are appropriate for your topic.

⦿ Search by call number: If you know the call number prefix for a certain section of the library in which you want to find a book, you can search this way. For example, if you wanted a book on the solar system, you could enter 520 into the search field, and it would bring up books on astronomy.

⦿ Search by keyword: If you can think of a keyword that might be in the title or description of a book you want to find, enter the word in the search field.

     0-7424-1953-3 *Complete Library Skills*

Boolean Searches

▶ **Using a search engine, enter the word *Michigan* into the search field. How many results come up? Too many to count?**

Sometimes you can use words to help define your search; in other words, to help get results that are more specific to the information you need. The words *and, or,* and *but not* are called **Boolean operators**. Using these words in a keyword search will help you narrow down your choices of web sites. Look at the example below:

Search for: | Peanut butter **and** jelly

⦿ AND   ◯ OR   ◯ BUT NOT

Your results would only mention both peanut butter and jelly.

Search for: | Peanut butter **or** jelly

◯ AND   ⦿ OR   ◯ BUT NOT

Your results would mention peanut butter, jelly, and both.

Search for: | Peanut butter **but not** jelly

◯ AND   ◯ OR   ⦿ BUT NOT

Your results would only mention peanut butter.

▶ **Perform the search below. Answer the questions.**

Search for: | Michigan **and** Great Lakes

⦿ AND   ◯ OR   ◯ BUT NOT

How did your results change from above? _____

_____

How did using a Boolean operator help you find exactly what you were looking for? _____

Name _____ Date _____

Those Little Words

Using Boolean operators (and, or, but not) can really affect the results of a search. It is a good idea to use them often so you get the best search results possible.

▶ **Use the following criteria to search on your library's electronic card catalog. Answer the questions below.**

Search for: | weather **but not** cold

○ AND   ○ OR   ● BUT NOT

What do you notice about the results of your search?

_____

Write ten book titles that appear in your results.

_____   _____

_____   _____

_____   _____

_____   _____

_____   _____

Now let's change your search by using a different Boolean operator.

Search for: | weather **and** cold

● AND   ○ OR   ○ BUT NOT

How have the results of your search changed?

_____

How can Boolean operators help you find information?

_____

Title Search

A title search is the most specific of all searches. When you perform a title search, you can leave off the words *the*, *a*, and *an*.

Tracy did a title search to find a book that she loves. She can't remember the exact title, but knows it has the word *summer* in it. She thinks the title might be *The Summer of Blue*, so she types the following in the title search:

Title Search   the summer of blue

▶ **Answer the questions about the title search above.**

1. What did Tracy do that was unnecessary? _____

2. Does it matter if you use capital letters when doing a search? Try it!

_____

Here are the results of Tracy's search. Answer the questions that follow.

Number	Title	Year
1	The Summer of Blue/Lillie Trevor Illustrated by Karen Lewis	2002
2	The Summer of Blue (videorecording) LDS Publications, Ltd.	2001
3	The Summer of Blue/Lillie Trevor	1999

3. Tracy is sure that the book she is thinking of has illustrations. Which record should she select? _____

4. What would Tracy find if she looked for record 2 on the library shelf?

_____

105   0-7424-1953-3 *Complete Library Skills*

Name _____ Date _____

Author Search

You're at your library's browser station and you want to search for the author Mike Pitts. Uh-oh! You entered Mike Pitts into the author search, and no records were found. The browser asks for **last name first**, so you retype his name, Pitts, Mike. Several books come up. You select the one you are most interested in—*All About Peaches.*

➤ **Below is the record that came up on the computer screen. Use it to answer the questions below.**

Author	Pitts, Mike
Title	All About Peaches
Pub Info	New York: Fruit Press, c2003.
Description	98 p. illus.
Location	580 Pi
Summary	This book includes facts about peach trees and peaches. It also includes information on growing and harvesting peaches.
Subject	Peaches—Juvenile nonfiction
Subject	Fruit—Juvenile literature

1. What year was the book published? _____

2. What is the call number? _____

3. How many pages are in the book? _____

4. Who is the publisher of the book? _____

Where is the publisher located? _____

5. If you were doing a report on growing fruit, would this book be

helpful? Explain. _____

_____

Name _____ Date _____

Subject Search

Even though you think they are fun to watch, the squirrels on the birdfeeder are driving your dad nuts. During your library time, you decide to find a book to help him get rid of them. You aren't sure where to start, so you do a subject search for "squirrels." Here is what comes up on your computer screen.

Number	Subjects (1–5 of 5)	Entries Found
1	Squirrels	11
2	Squirrel Control	4
3	Squirrel Humor	3
4	Squirrel Fiction	8
5	Squirrel Noise Recordings	1

▶ **Read the search results. Answer the questions below.**

1. Which of the subjects above best narrows your search?

_____

2. Which other subject might have helpful information?

_____

After making your selection, another screen comes up. Use it to answer the question that follows.

Number	Title (1–2 of 2)	Year
1	Outwitting Squirrels	2001
2	Techniques for Trapping Squirrels	1999

3. Which of the above titles would you choose to help your dad?

Explain. _____

Name _____   Date _____

Keyword Search

Jamal loves tennis. He knows that he should type in the word *tennis,* but he's not sure whether a subject search or a keyword search would be better. So he tries both ways.

The keyword search returned over 200 records! The subject search returned over 80 records! Since he's not sure of the exact subject he's interested in, he goes back to the keyword search. This time he uses a suggestion on the screen and types *tennis AND training.* Ah-ha! A list of only 8 titles comes up. Much better!

➤ **Answer the questions below based on Jamal's experience with searches.**

1. Which appears to be more accurate, a subject search or a keyword search? _____

2. Why did adding the word *AND* help Jamal find what he was looking for? _____

3. What do you think would have happened if Jamal entered *tennis BUT NOT training*?

    _____

4. A keyword search looks over the entire record for a word, but a subject search looks only in the subject headings for the word. When might a keyword search be more helpful? When might a subject search be more helpful? Explain. _____

    _____

    _____

Internet Searches

Searching the Internet is similar to searching your library's card catalog, but Internet results can include almost everything that is available on the Web. Internet searches use a search engine to look for sites that match the words you enter into the search field. Your school librarian can help you find the best search engine to use.

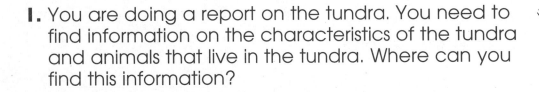

▶ **Look at the searches below. Think of the words you would use to find this information. Underline the words you would enter into the search field. Using a search engine, enter these words into the search field. Write the name of a website that the search engine finds to answer your question. If possible, print the home page for each website you write below.**

1. You are doing a report on the tundra. You need to find information on the characteristics of the tundra and animals that live in the tundra. Where can you find this information?

    _____

2. Where can you learn about gravity?

    _____

    _____

3. Where can you find out what the weather is like right now in Puerto Rico?

    _____

    _____

4. Where can you find out how the rake was invented?

    _____

    _____

Internet Searches

➡ **Ask your librarian to help you find the best search engine to use. Then see if you can find a website to answer each of the questions below. Write the words you would search with on the first line. Then write the name of the website on the second line. If you have access to a printer, print each page as you find it.**

1. Where could you learn about Paul Revere and his famous ride?

_____

_____

2. Where could you learn about haiku and see examples of haiku?

_____

_____

3. Where could you look to find information on different traditions celebrated in December?

_____

_____

4. Where could you look to learn all about China—its population, size, products, climate?

_____

_____

5. Where could you look to learn all about Earth Day?

_____

_____

EARTH DAY EVERY DAY

Name _____ Date _____

Is It Any Good?

Not all websites are created equal. How do you know whether the site you are using is a good source to use for information? First you should think about your purpose for searching the web. Are you looking for something fun to do? Are you writing a report for class? It's much more important to use quality sources for a report than it is for something you're doing for fun.

▶ **Study the chart below. It will give you some ideas about what to look for when evaluating websites. Use it to answer questions on the next page.**

Good Sources
- no typing mistakes
- easy to read and understand; graphics are clear and add to the content of the site
- include in-depth information
- not biased; contain objective facts
- updated often; current information
- from a reliable source; you've heard of the organization that created the page (a URL ending with **.gov**, **.edu**, or **.org** is also a good sign)
- stable; the pages stick around for a long time and are always there when you go back to them

Not-So-Good Sources
- contain typing mistakes
- difficult to read; graphics are distracting
- information is not in-depth or accurate
- it shows only one person's opinions
- page hasn't been updated in a long time
- you've never heard of the organization that created the page
- here today, gone tomorrow; page is not there when you look a few months later

Name _____ Date _____

Which Should I Use?

1. You are trying to find help with fractions. Which of
   the following web sites would be the best
   source? Circle your choice. Explain why you
   chose it on the line.
   a. www.mathiseasy.com
   b. www.library.org/math
   c. www.fredsfractions.com

   _____

2. You want to learn all about the United States
   Presidents. Which of the computer screens below
   looks more factual? Circle the source you would use.

   > a. The Presidents of the United States
   >   Listing by year   Listing by name
   >   Famous Facts About Presidents
   >   Presidential Portrait Gallery
   >
   >   The White House
   >   last updated April 2004

   > b. All About President of U.S.
   >   Click here! For a list of all the Presidence
   >   The best president was John F. Kennedy
   >   My gallery of president pictures
   >   last updated October 1998

3. Your friend Carlos needs help finding information for a
   report that is due in two weeks. Make a "Best of the Web"
   list for Carlos of the four most reputable websites you know
   of where he can find information.

   _____   _____

   _____   _____

 0-7424-1953-3 *Complete Library Skills*

Which Is the Best?

▶ **Read each of the research projects below. Decide which website would be the best site to use to find the information you need. Circle the right choice. Then write why you chose that site on the line. Use the chart on page 111 for help.**

1. You are doing a project on **manatees** for class.

   a. Megan's Manatee Home Page
      http://www.megansmanatees.com

   b. Save the Manatee
      http://www.manatee.org

   c. Amazing Mammal Facts
      http://www.mammalfacts.ca.com/whales

_____

2. You are doing a report on the state of **Oklahoma**. You need to learn all about its size, population, location, climate, and state bird.

   a. Oklahoma! The Musical
      http://www.singalong.com/broadway

   b. Oklahoma Facts
      http://www.50states.com/Oklahoma

   c. Tornado Alley
      http://www.oklahomatwisters.com

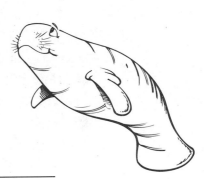

_____

3. Your career day report is on being a **reporter**.

   a. Career Information Online
      http://www.mcl.careerinfo.org/reporter

   b. Get All the Facts
      http://www.juicystories.com/celebrities

   c. Be a Reporter
      http://www.uaskthequestions.com/school

_____

0-7424-1953-3 *Complete Library Skills*

Which Should I Choose?

➡️ **Look at the research situations below. Choose which site you think would be best to use to find the right information. Circle the best site. Then write why you chose that site on the line.**

1. You are making a human skeleton out of construction paper and brads for a presentation in class. But you're not sure if all of the parts are labeled correctly.

   a. The Human Skeleton
   http://www.science.org/anatomy/skeleton

   b. My Wiggly Body
   http://www.jasonsbones.com/femur

   c. Skeletons and Other Creepy Halloween Costumes
   http://www.frightnight.com/costumes

   _____

2. One of your books has a big silver seal on the cover. It says *Newbery Award*. Your librarian wants you to find out some information about this award and tell your class about it.

   a. Best of Children's Books
   http://www.libpage.com/george/best/newbery

   b. History of Children's Book Awards
   http://www.bookawards.com/newbery/tommy

   c. The Newbery Award
   http://www.ala.org/alsc/newbery.html

   _____

3. Your science fair project is due in two weeks and you haven't even started! You need some science fair project ideas.

   a. A Science Fair Project Resource Guide
   http://www.ipl.org/youth/projectguide

   b. Complete Guide to Science Projects
   http://www.members.web.com/ScienceFair/explosiveideas

   c. The Kid's Guide to Hands-On Science
   http://www.ucandoscience.com

   _____

Name _____ Date _____

Match the Web Sites

Some websites are good to use when you need to collect facts for a project or report. Other websites are just for fun.

▶ **Look at each website below. Does the website sound like it is for fun or for learning about a subject? Match the website to the reason you would choose it. Write the letter on the line.**

Panda Bears

1. http://www.giantpanda.org _____

2. http://www.nationalzoo.com/mammals/giantpanda/

view _____

3. http://www.art.com/buy/mammals/panda _____

    a. You want to watch the pandas at the zoo feed on bamboo

    b. You want to buy a panda poster for your little sister

    c. You want to learn how to help save pandas from extinction

Literature

4. http://www.childrensbooks.com/authors/paterson _____

5. http://www.umich.edu/recommend/books _____

6. http://www.writeapoem.com/suggestions/topics _____

    d. You want some help coming up with poetry topics

    e. You want to learn about your favorite author, Katherine Paterson

    f. You want some suggestions on new books to read

Encyclo-readia Book Project

Project Description
Students will research a topic of interest. Using their research, each student will write a report about the topic. Students will submit their reports, along with illustrations, to bind up in a classroom book.

Materials Needed
Supply a graphic organizer, such as a web or note cards, on which students will record their notes. Demonstration on how to correctly use the graphic organizer might be valuable if it is new to the students.

Introducing the Project
It is very important that students learn to write research papers without copying words exactly as they appear in a source. This is a good time to teach appropriate note taking by doing a demonstration of using the graphic organizer. Select a short piece of informational text. Guide students in breaking down the text into categories. Then show students how to pull information from the text and use it to create words and short phrases. Next, have them remove the research material from their desks and ask them to write original sentences using the information from their graphic organizers. This is also a good time to model good paragraph writing, using topic sentences and supporting details.

Classroom Connections
Reviewing the concept of fact and opinion might help students when they are filling in their graphic organizers with facts from their research materials. Turn your classroom lesson into a game of "Simon Says." Create a signal for fact (hand on top of head) and opinion (hand over heart). Choose a student to be Simon. Have the student say to the class, "Simon **knows** …" (for a fact) and "Simon **thinks** …" (for an opinion). For example, "Simon thinks that winter is the best season," or "Simon knows that winter is a season." The first person that Simon sees moving his or her hand incorrectly becomes Simon for the next round.

Display and Presentation
Compile the projects into a book called "Encyclo-readia Volume I" or "Our Class Encyclo-readia." Have students design a cover and bind the pages, or use a three-ring binder with a cover pocket to display student-made covers one at a time.

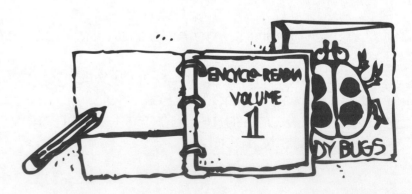

0-7424-1953-3 Complete Library Skills

Name _____ Date _____

Encyclo-readia

Genre: Nonfiction
Due Date: _____

Dear Third Graders,

Learning something new is so much fun! You will be choosing a topic that interests you for the focus of your research and writing for a book project. Using your research, you will write a short report on your topic. We will compile a classroom encyclo-readia.

Materials Needed
Graphic organizer for note taking; pen; computer; paper; crayons or markers

Project Requirements

1. Think about several topics that interest you. Write them down on a sheet of paper. In the library, find books on the topics you wrote down. Choose the topic that interests you the most. Also make sure that there are enough research materials on that topic that you can use.

2. While you are reading, use your graphic organizer to take notes.
- Write your topic at the top of the page.
- Choose three subtopics, and write them in your organizer.
- Under your subtopics, record words and phrases that relate to each subtopic. Try to use five words or fewer for each point.

3. Put your research material away before you start writing.

4. Next, write a paragraph about each subtopic. Each paragraph should have a topic sentence, followed by supporting details.

5. Write an introductory paragraph. This will be first on your page. Edit and recopy your subtopic paragraphs to follow your introduction.

6. Now write a concluding paragraph. This will sum up the information on your page.

7. You may add pictures or a border to your finished page. Be sure to put your "by line" (by <u>your name</u>) on the page.

Here's your schedule for the encyclo-readia project:

Check When Done

☐ Week 1—Choose your topic. Also choose the books you will use and have them approved by your teacher.

☐ Week 2—Read your research materials and take notes on your graphic organizer.

☐ Week 3—Put research materials away and draft your paragraphs.

☐ Week 4—Have an adult help you edit your paragraphs. Create a finished report and illustrate it.

What You Will Turn In
Each student will turn in his or her research project with illustrations. These will be bound together into a classroom book. We will work together on cover designs, and the book will be placed in our classroom library for reference.

Encyclo-readia Evaluation

How did your book project go? Are you happy with the results? Did you enjoy learning more about the topic that you chose?

▶ **Evaluate how you did by filling in the chart below.**

Criteria	Excellent	Good	Fair	Needs Improvement
My written work is well-organized, neat, and accurate.				
My written work is my own and original.				
I included facts and examples to support my writing.				
I used multiple research materials when collecting data.				
My project completely meets project requirements.				

Project was turned in on time ☐ Yes ☐ No

Project Designer's Tag

Name _____

Date _____

Topic _____

Types of research materials used

_____

_____

I'm the Expert Book Project

Project Description

Each student will read a nonfiction book for the purpose of learning a new skill—performing a science experiment, mastering an art or craft, preparing a recipe, or learning a physical skill such as karate or dance. After reading the book, the student will prepare written instructions to teach the class the new skill. The student will also demonstrate the new skill to the class.

Materials Needed

All materials will come from home. You may need to help students who are struggling with unusual materials or demonstrations.

Introducing the Project

As a class, brainstorm interesting things the class would like to know how to do. Be sure to share topics that interest you, as well. Guide students toward books that will help them become experts on new topics. At the end of the first week, model a presentation for the class, demonstrating a new skill that you learned by reading a nonfiction book.

Classroom Connections

Clear, understandable instructions are important to have when trying to learn a new skill. We encounter instructions all the time in our daily lives. Have students brainstorm the ways in which we encounter instructions in our lives. Generate a list. Then ask students to talk with their parents and family members about the types of directions or instructions they encounter at work or home—using computer manuals, following recipes, making home repairs, using an automatic teller machine. Ask students to write down and bring in three examples they came up with when talking with their families. Make additions to the list. Students will be impressed as the list grows and grows.

Presenting the New Skill

Each student will demonstrate the new skill that he or she has learned. Use an overhead transparency to display the directions or instructions that each student created for his or her presentation so other students can follow along or write them down. Or, if you wish, you can copy each set of instructions, bind them into a book, and hand out a copy to each student or place one copy in your classroom library for reference.

Name _____ Date _____

My Favorite Books

1. _____
                                    Title

_____   _____   _____
Call Number   Author   Genre

2. _____
                                    Title

_____   _____   _____
Call Number   Author   Genre

3. _____
                                    Title

_____   _____   _____
Call Number   Author   Genre

4. _____
                                    Title

_____   _____   _____
Call Number   Author   Genre

5. _____
                                    Title

_____   _____   _____
Call Number   Author   Genre

6. _____
                                    Title

_____   _____   _____
Call Number   Author   Genre

 0-7424-1953-3 *Complete Library Skills*

Newbery and Caldecott Book Award Winners

The following lists highlight the last 15 years of Newbery and Caldecott award winners.

Newbery Award Winners

2003: Crispin: The Cross of Lead by Avi
2002: A Single Shard by Park, Linda Sue
2001: A Year Down Yonder by Peck, Richard
2000: Bud, Not Buddy by Curtis, Christopher Paul
1999: Holes by Sachar, Louis
1998: Out of the Dust by Hesse, Karen
1997: The View from Saturday by Konigsburg, E. L.
1996: The Midwife's Apprentice by Cushman, Karen
1995: Walk Two Moons by Creech, Sharon
1994: The Giver by Lowry, Lois
1993: Missing May by Rylant, Cynthia
1992: Shiloh by Naylor, Phyllis Reynolds
1991: Maniac Magee by Spinelli, Jerry
1990: Number the Stars by Lowry, Lois
1989: Joyful Noise: Poems for Two Voices by Fleischman, Paul

Caldecott Award Winners

2003: My Friend Rabbit by Rohmann, Eric
2002: The Three Pigs by Wiesner, David
2001: So You Want to Be President? by Small, David
2000: Joseph Had a Little Overcoat by Taback, Simms
1999: Snowflake Bentley by Azarian, Mary
1998: Rapunzel by Zelinsky, Paul O.
1997: Golem by Wisniewski, David
1996: Officer Buckle and Gloria by Rathmann, Peggy
1995: Smoky Night by Diaz, David
1994: Grandfather's Journey by Say, Allen
1993: Mirette on the High Wire by McCully, Emily Arnold
1992: Tuesday by Wiesner, David
1991: Black and White by Macaulay, David
1990: Lon Po Po: A Red-Riding Hood Story from China by Young, Ed
1989: Song and Dance Man by Gammell, Stephen

Amber Brown Is Not a Crayon by Danziger, Paula

Boxcar Children by Warner, Gertrude Chandler

Brave Kids: Cora Frear by Goodman, Susan E.

Buffalo Bill and the Pony Express by Coerr, Eleanor

Charlotte's Web by White, E. B.

Chocolate Fever by Smith, Robert Kimmel

Encyclopedia Brown, Boy Detective by Sobol, Donald J.

Fantastic Mr. Fox by Dahl, Roald

Flat Stanley by Brown, Jeff

Hank the Cowdog #01: The Original Adventures by Erickson, John R.

How to Eat Fried Worms by Rockwell, Thomas

Knights of the Kitchen Table by Scieszka, Jon

Mr. Popper's Penguins by Atwater, Richard and Florence

My Father's Dragon by Gannett, Ruth Stiles

No Flying in the House by Brock, Betty

Not My Dog by Radowsky, Colby F.

Ramona Quimby, Age 8 by Cleary, Beverly

Rats on the Roof and Other Stories by Marshall, James

Sideways Stories from Wayside School by Sachar, Louis

The Adventures of Captain Underpants by Pilkey, Dav

The Chronicles of Narnia Boxed Set by Lewis, C. S.

The Dragonling by Koller, Jackie

The Fairy Rebel by Banks, Lynne Reid

The Houdini Box by Selznick, Brian

The Invasion (Animorphs) by Applegate, Katherine

The Stories Julian Tells by Cameron, Ann

Glossary

almanac—a book filled with fun facts and interesting information that is printed yearly

atlas—a book of maps

autobiography—a book that is written by the person that it is about

author card—The author card begins with the author's last name. This is the first line on the card.

bibliography—a list of resources that were used for information

biography—A book that is written about someone's life. It is written by someone other than whom the book is about.

book spine—The book spine is the outside edge of the book. It has the call number printed on it. This is what you see when you look at books on a shelf.

Caldecott Medal—a medal awarded yearly to the artist of the most distinguished American picture book

call number—This can be found on the spine of the book. It shows you where you can find a book in the library. Fiction call numbers start with an *F*. Nonfiction call numbers start with a three-digit prefix.

catalog card—This card shows the author of the book, title of the book, publishing information, copyright date, illustration information, and number of pages in the book. Other information may also be printed on the card.

copyright date—this is the date the book was printed

Dewey Decimal Classification® system—a system of organizing nonfiction books by subject created in 1876 by Melvin Dewey

dictionary—a book of definitions

encyclopedia—a set of books that holds general information on thousands of subjects

fairytales/folktales—Stories that have been passed down orally from one generation to another. They often feature good vs. evil.

fantasy—a story that takes place in an imaginary world and cannot really happen

fiction—fiction books are make-believe books that come out of the author's imagination

graphic organizer—a type of note-taking format that helps you see relationships between words and facts; webs, charts, Venn diagrams, and timelines

guide words—words found at the top of a page in a reference book to help you find a word you are looking for

historical fiction—a make-believe story that features historical elements, such as the setting or characters

illustration—pictures and art within a book

informational—books filled with factual information on a specific topic

Internet—a system of networks that connects computers around the world

magazine—A short collection of stories or articles. It is usually published once a month.

Newbery Award—a medal awarded yearly to the author of the most distinguished American story book

nonfiction—A nonfiction book tells a true story. The story is based on facts and can be about many different subjects.

poetry—A written piece that can be silly, serious, sad, or funny. Usually it rhymes, but it doesn't have to.

publisher—The group of people who create the book. They print it and put it together.

realistic fiction—a make-believe story that has the potential of being real

search engine—a software program that searches and gathers information that is about a certain subject

subject—this is what the book is about

subject card—The subject card begins with the subject of the book. It is shown in capital letters.

table of contents—found at the beginning of a book, it shows you the title of each chapter or page in a book

thesaurus—A book that shows multiple ways to say something. It shows synonyms and antonyms for common, overused words.

title card—The title card begins with the title of a book. This is the first line on the card.

title page—Found in the front of the book, this page shows the title, author, illustrator, and publishing information.

Answer Key

What's in a Library? 6
1. Libraries
2. fiction
3. real
4. subject
5. magazines

Mother May I? 7
Reasons under library monitor
How to care for plants
Find a book to take home
Learn about Chicago, Illinois
Reasons under traffic stopper
Run around and scream
Practice basketball moves
Draw on and rip pages

What's in a Title? 8
1. Goldie Bubble
2. How to Avoid Cats
3. Swishy Tail
4. Wave Press
5. Fish Bowl, Florida
6. fiction

**Using a Table
of Contents** 9
1. page 10
2. 7 chapters
3. Tornadoes and Hurricanes
4. page 50
5. 7 pages
6. Weather Begins with the Sun
7. Chapter 6, Clouds
8. more than 50 pages

The Table Tells a Lot 10
1. 5 chapters
2. Chapter 4, The Smartest
   Reptiles
3. page 1
4. Chapter 5, The Future of
   Turtles and Tortoises in
   Space
5. 8 pages

**Choose Your
Books Wisely** 12
1. e
2. d
3. c
4. f
5. a
6. b

Who Needs It? 14
Books that the girl needs
How to Start a Bug Collection
101 Kinds of Bugs
Butterfly Basics
Books that the boy wants

Bugs Live, in Concert
The Mammoth Mosquito
The Day I Became Dessert

Out of Order 15
Correct order of books
Row 1: Al, Br, Ch, Ga, Ju, Mo, Th,
       Yo, Zi
Row 2: Ba, Ci, De, Fl, Ho, Ka, Nu,
       Pl, Sl
Row 3: Ac, Br, Bu, Da, Di, Ey, Ha,
       Tr, Wa

**Alphabetical
Challenge** 16
Correct order: cabbage,
ebony, erode, final, hospital,
host, jolt, judge, justice, method,
minimum, paste, quip, radio,
range, rare, satellite, satire,
saturate, yearn
Answer to riddle: A bristlecone
pine tree

Poppy's Problem 17
Correct order: pace, pack,
patient, peddle, pending,
phantom, phone, phonics, picnic,
planet, plant, pleasant, please,
plight, plow, posture, price,
proof, prop, pupil, put, pylon

**Fiction or
Nonfiction?** 21
1. fiction
2. nonfiction
3. nonfiction
4. fiction
5. nonfiction
6. nonfiction
7. nonfiction
8. fiction

Call Me! 23
1. Sn
2. Re
3. So
4. Sh
5. Co
6. St
7. Bu
8. Tr
9. Bu

Order Up! 24
1. Ba, Ra, Za
2. Ab, Eb, Ob
3. An, On, Sn
4. Ro, To, Zo
5. At, It, St
6. Di, Ji, Wi

7. Br, To, Tr
8. Di, Mi, Pi
9. Lu, Mu, Pu
10. Ha, Ma, Na

Musical Books 25
1. F Jo, F Lo, F Po
2. F Gl, F Kl, F Sl
3. F Hi, F Mi, F Ri
4. F De, F He, F Me
5. F Ba, F Ma F Za
6. F Br, F Fr, F Gr

**Arrange the
Nonfiction Books** 28
Column 1: 300 Ad, 400 Ta, 600
          St, 800 Bl, 900 Br
Column 2: 200 Be, 300 Sr, 400
          Wa, 500 Al, 600 Re
Column 3: 200 Cr, 400 Jo, 500
          Ho, 700 Fl, 900 De
Column 4: 410 Ma, 420 Fl, 450 Fr,
          470 Bu, 470 Sr
Column 5: 830 Gu, 850 Th, 870
          Me, 890 Bu, 890 Ze

Which Comes First? 29
Column 1: 533 Jo, 533 Tr, 535 St,
          536 Or, 537 Ke
Column 2: 963 Bl, 964 Ta, 965
          Ad, 965 Br, 967 St
Column 3: 751 Ca, 752 He, 757
          Br, 759 Ab, 759 Pe
Column 4: 152 Ei, 384 Ru, 432 Ki,
          565 Th, 974 Om
Column 5: 384 Ca, 499 Sh, 499
          Zo, 565 Br, 962 Je

Reading a Card 32
1. F Po
2. The Forgetful Frog
3. Pamela Pond
4. Marsh, New York
5. Bog Press
6. 2003
7. yes
8. It's a story about a frog who
   forgets everything.
9. fiction
10. title card

Reading a Card 33
1. F Ro
2. The Dinosaur Next Door
3. Pete Rock
4. 80 pages
5. It's a story about a
   neighborhood dinosaur.
6. Rockville, New Jersey
7. fiction
8. yes

9. 2003
10. Stone Press

Reading a Card 34
1. The Seal Who Couldn't Swim
2. F Fi
3. fiction
4. James Fin
5. 45 pages
6. 2003
7. It's a story about a seal who can't swim.
8. yes
9. seals
10. subject card

Using a Dictionary 36
spill, R–Z; bargain, A–H; February, A–H; umbrella, R–Z; piano, I–Q; eagle, A–H; joke, I–Q; money, I–Q

Crossing Guards 37
Across
3. tug
6. carrot
7. easy
9. rusty
12. kick
Down
1. story
2. picture
4. gate
5. many
8. ankle
10. sand
11. yams

Words in alphabetical order:
ankle, carrot, easy, gate, kick, king, many, picture, sand, story, tug, yams

No Beans About It 38
1. after
2. before
3. before
4. on
5. on
6. before
7. after
8. before
9. on
10. after
11. after
12. on
13. before
14. before
15. on
16. after
17. on
18. after

Now That's Salty! 39
1. before
2. after
3. on
4. on
5. after
6. before
7. on
8. after
Answer to question: the Dead Sea

Summer Syllables 40
1. one syllable
2. three syllables
3. one syllable
4. two syllables
5. three syllables
6. two syllables
7. two syllables
8. three syllables
Math answer: 9, (3 x 2) + 3 = 9

Sylla-Graph 41
watermelon–four syllables
breakfast–two syllables
servant–two syllables
buffalo–three syllables
arch–one syllable
aggressive–three syllables
victim–two syllables
column–two syllables
history–three syllables
significant–four syllables
margin–two syllables
debilitate–four syllables
pilot–two syllables
compulsory–four syllables
cucumber–three syllables
leisure–two syllables
sketch–one syllable

What Kind of Word Is It? 42
1. noun, verb
2. to copy or mimic
3. a boot with a metal blade/ wheels or a large fish in the ray family
4. three
5. Answers will vary.

A Fly with Many Meanings 43
1. four
2. four
3. eight
Definition numbers for story:
3, 3, 6, 5, 2, 7

Words in the Round 44
Nouns: rabbit, history, puppy, bird, dew, hobby, dime, motel
Verbs: sweep, buy, go, say, grow
Both: color, sail, draw, hand, trap, mop, waste

Animal Crackers 45
One-syllable words: time, host, end
Two-syllable words: basket, linger, utter, escape
Three-syllable words: wallpaper, holiday, aggravate, library, energy
Animal question: the blue whale

Where Would You Look? 47
1. Volume 1
2. Volume 2
3. Volume 17
4. Volume 3
5. Volume 8
6. Volume 5
7. Volume 6
8. Volume 6
9. Volume 18
10. Volume 9
11. Volume 10
12. Volume 4
There are 20 volumes.

A Wealth of Information 48
1. Volume 5
2. Volume 7
3. Volume 2
4. Volume 13
5. Volume 15
6. Volume 6
7. Volume 16
8. Volume 15
9. Volume 9
10. Volume 7
11. Volume 19
12. Volume 15

So Much Information 49
1. d
2. b
3. a
4. e
5. c
6. h
7. f
8. g

Answer Key

Volumes of Information........50
Subjects found in Volume C:
Chile, capillary, Anton Chekhov, cement
Subjects found in Volume L:
licorice, legume, Madeleine L'Engle
Subjects found in Volume M:
Mayflower Compact, Mount Rushmore, Massasoit

U.S. States and Presidents 54
Across
4. wheat
5. cardinal
6. Hudson
7. Virginia
8. Taft
9. Oklahoma
10. Rhode Island
Down
1. Nashville
2. Frankfort
3. Raleigh

Online Almanacs 60
1. Scientists estimate the universe began 13 to 15 billion years ago.
2. He opened a men's clothing store, acted as judge in Jackson Co., MO, and was elected to U.S. Senate.
3. Karl Malone (Utah)
4. Whitcomb L. Judson
All other answers will vary.

Exploring Egypt 62
Some may have more than one source
Orange canteens: the spelling of *mummification*, parts of speech of *desert*
Blue canteens: the life of King Tut, background information on the pyramids
Red canteen: another word for *hot*
Green canteens: physical features of Sahara Desert, the location of Egypt on a map
Yellow canteens: the weather in Egypt, the population of Egypt

Exploring the Sciences..........74
1. 598
2. 599
3. 595
4. 597
5. 599
6. 595
7. 593
8. 594
9. 592
10. 597
11. 594
12. 590

Match the Dewey 75
The Invention of the Paper Clip—670
Journey Through the Solar System—523
Famous Poems—808
World Religions—291
Ancient Roman Art—709
Let's Learn French—448
All About the Mind—150
Training to Be a Soldier—355
Antarctica at a Glance—919

Biographies and Autobiographies 78
My Life as a Carpenter—autobiography
The 36th President of the United States—biography
I Won One Million Dollars!—autobiography
Bill Lawson—A Life in Exile—biography
Everyone Wants My Job—autobiography
Katy's Life—biography
Cynthia Chandelier—Exposed—biography
Searching for My Mother—autobiography

Is It Real?.............................83
Realistic fiction books: *I'm Grounded!, One Cold, Wintry Day*

Title Search.........................105
1. Tracy didn't have to include the word *the*.
2. It does not matter if you use capital letters.
3. Tracy should choose record 1.
4. She would find a video.

Author Search 106
1. 2003
2. 580 Pi
3. 98 pages
4. Fruit Press, New York
5. Yes, it has information about growing peaches.

Subject Search 107
1. Squirrel control
2. Squirrels
3. Answers will vary.

Keyword Search 108
1. a subject search
2. The word *AND* required the results to have both words in the title.
3. None of the results would have included the word *training* in the title.
4. A keyword search is useful when you're not quite sure what you are looking for, but you have an idea. A subject search is useful when you know you want information within a certain subject.

Which Should I Use? 112
1. b; .org is a good indication that it is a reputable site
2. a

Which Is the Best?..............113
1. b; .org is a good indication that it is a reputable site
2. b; the other two sites are not general sites about Oklahoma
3. a; this site has information about different careers, the other two sites do not

Which Should I Choose?....114
1. a; .org is a good indication that this site is reputable
2. c; the other two sites are people's personal sites
3. a; the other two sites do not seem reputable

Match the Web Sites 115
1. c
2. a
3. b
4. e
5. f
6. d